Washington Wine Country

John Doerper
Photography by Greg Vaughn

COMPASS AMERICAN GUIDES
An imprint of Fodor's Travel Publications

Compass American Guides: Washington Wine Country

Editor: Craig Seligman
Designer: Tina R. Malaney
Compass Editorial Director: Daniel Mangin
Compass Creative Director: Fabrizio La Rocca
Compass Senior Editor: Kristin Moehlmann
Production Editor: Linda Schmidt
Photo Editor and Archival Researcher: Melanie Marin
Map Design: Mark Stroud, Moon Street Cartography

Cover photo by Greg Vaughn

First Edition
ISBN 1–4000–1374–7
ISSN 1547–8734

Compass American Guides, 1745 Broadway, New York, NY 10019
PRINTED IN SINGAPORE

10 9 8 7 6 5 4 3 2 1

To Victoria, who has sustained me on my enological journeys.

C O N T E N T S

(top) The first step toward great wine is a sturdy vine. (Brent Bergherm)
(following spread) Seven Hills Vineyard. (Brent Bergherm)

Sidebars

Maps

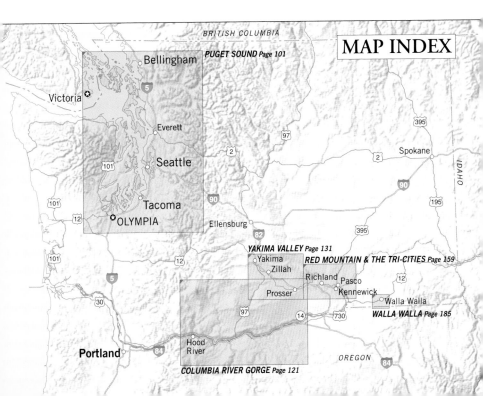

MAP INDEX

BRITISH COLUMBIA

PUGET SOUND Page 101

Bellingham

Victoria

Everett

Seattle

Tacoma

OLYMPIA

Ellensburg

Spokane

IDAHO

YAKIMA VALLEY Page 131

Yakima

Zillah

RED MOUNTAIN & THE TRI-CITIES Page 159

Richland Pasco

Prosser Kennewick

Walla Walla

WALLA WALLA Page 185

Portland

Hood River

COLUMBIA RIVER GORGE Page 121

OREGON

INTRODUCTION

This 1850 engraving shows roads leading to Fort Vancouver and the Columbia River beyond.

THE SUN SHINES BRIGHTLY, its light bouncing off the surface of Lake Wallula in silver sparkles. Far below my rocky perch, flying very low and almost touching the placid waters of the Columbia River (blocked downstream by McNary Dam and known here as Lake Wallula), a white pelican flies upstream, searching, perhaps, for its fishing buddies—since white pelicans, unlike their brown coastal cousins, are communal fishers. The terns are more energetic, hovering high in the sky and suddenly plunging, head first, when they spot a fish below the surface. As soon as a tern rises with a fish in its bill, a family of gulls takes off in loud pursuit. But the terns usually make a clean getaway.

The heat of the day releases the pungent aromas of sagebrush and dry herbs, the scent of spice and a faint whiff of roses. A light wind blows up dust devils. The breeze feels refreshingly cool, though it has traveled some 300 miles from the Pacific Ocean. As the wind picks up, clouds fan out over the sky, but the temperature doesn't drop. It looks like we may get one of the violent thunderstorms for which this area is famous.

About 200 years ago, on a site now submerged under Lake Wallula, Lewis and Clark camped down below, as did the Astorians and members of the Hudson's Bay Company a few miles upstream, where Fort Walla Walla stood on another now-submerged site. When the explorers passed through the region, they complained about the lack of firewood and the dearth of good food.

I'm certainly eating better than Lewis and Clark did, though my fare is less exotic. By the time the great explorers reached the Columbia, they had developed a taste for . . . dog. I'm happier with the flavorful smoked local salmon a winemaker gave me earlier this afternoon, accompanied by bread from a small bakery and a hunk of cheese from a winery deli. I enhance my meal with a glass of estate-grown cabernet sauvignon whose beautiful, supple body seems to incorporate the subtle wild aromas of the basalt cliffs and sagebrush slopes.

The sky has grown ominously dark. I'm wondering whether I should have an apple for dessert when my picnic is interrupted by a thunderclap. My car is only a few feet away; I manage to stow the food and wine and my blanket just as the heavy drops start to fall. Within minutes, sheets of rain have blotted out the tall cliffs across the river, and bolts of lightning are flashing across the roiling waters.

The tempest prompts me to reflect on what the scene must have looked like 12,000 years ago, when perhaps the largest floods the world has ever seen roared through this gap. The floods—known variously as the Spokane, Bretz, or Missoula Floods, depending on who's writing—were triggered when a huge body of water trapped in western Montana by a cordilleran ice sheet crashed through and rushed downriver, breaking over the rim of the Columbia Plateau near Spokane and heading toward the ocean, only to be slowed by the narrow Wallula Gap, where the Columbia River had earlier forced its way through an 1,100-foot-high ridge of the Horse Heaven Hills.

The flood's horrendous current moved a truly gigantic amount of water. When it backed up, it formed the vast if temporary Lake Lewis, which stretched up the Yakima River Valley to the site of the current city of Yakima, through the Walla Walla Valley to the Blue Mountains, and up again along the Snake River to its junction with the Salmon. At its fullest, Lake Lewis was about 800 feet deep, and it discharged through the gap at a rate of 18 cubic miles per hour and at a speed of 40 miles per hour.

But, as big as it was, the lake lasted only a few hours before the floodwaters had cleared the gap and rushed on to widen and deepen the Columbia River Gorge, 140 miles downstream. Yet these waters, however briefly arrested in their flight by the gap, dropped vast amounts of alluvial deposits—which today make up the deep, well-drained, grape-friendly soils of the Columbia, Walla Walla, and Yakima Valleys. The Wallula Gap, marking the confluence of the three rivers that run through these valleys, is the heart of these three superb grape-growing regions.

The rain subsides. Though I'm surrounded by sagebrush, now returned to dim visibility in the gloom, I know that the Wallula Gap is close to another important boundary, the one that separates the sagebrush steppe, which runs west from here to the eastern foothills of the Cascade Mountains, and the short-grass steppe, which extends east from the nearby hills to the western foothills of the Rocky Mountains. The change in vegetation marks the difference in annual rainfall. The grasslands to the east lie beyond the rain shadow of the Cascades, which block moisture from the sagebrush slopes to the west. Though irrigation is necessary for agriculture to succeed in the Columbia and Yakima Valleys, it's optional in the Puget Sound area and in the Walla Walla Valley, where rainfall is heavier.

■ FROM SAGEBRUSH TO GRAPEVINES

According to Ronald J. Taylor and Rolf W. Valum in their fine book *Sagebrush Country*, "the height and uniformity of growth" of tall sagebrush (*Artemesia tridentata*), the indicator species of the region, "can be used as a measure of cultivation potential assuming irrigation capabilities." Furthermore, they advise, "if the plants average approximately three feet or more in height the soil may be considered productively arable." Tall sagebrush has become scarce in some places for precisely that reason: it has been plowed up and replaced with field crops, orchards, and vineyards. But it persists at the margins of civilization, as in this mountain gap, where it still provides shelter and food to wild animals.

The first time I encountered this sagebrush, it gave me quite a jolt. On my first drive across the Cascade Mountains to eastern Washington's Wine Country, more than two decades ago, I was on a quest: I wanted to learn where and how some of the great wines I had recently tasted were made. Entering the Yakima Valley from the Cascades' sagebrush-covered foothills, I had serious doubts that wine this good could really come from so barren a region.

But as I reached the lower slopes of the hills, the barrenness gave way to verdant fields and orchards. Now the landscape seemed almost *too* lush for great vineyards. But I soon learned that the delicious wines produced here are no illusion. All day long, I sniffed and sipped and tasted. Wines from the barrel, wines from the bottle, wines with some age on them. Red wines, white wines, dessert wines. I was impressed. Later in the day, I visited the vineyards, walking along the rows of vines and picking up a handful of soil now and then—the very alluvium deposited thousands of years ago by those huge glacial floods pouring out of Montana. As the loose soil ran through my fingers, I became convinced that this region could indeed produce great wines. Since those days, vineyards have proliferated not only in the Yakima Valley and in the neighboring Columbia and Walla Walla Valleys, but also in western Washington.

(above) In this photograph taken in the 1920s, a man revels in the abundance of grapes in the Yakima Valley. (following pages) Hot-air ballooning is a popular recreational activity in the wine regions of eastern Washington.

The viticultural settings of Washington vary greatly. (Brent Bergherm)

There's plenty to do in eastern Washington's Wine Country beyond tasting wine. You can water-ski in summer and snowboard or ski from late fall through early spring, or head for the Columbia Gorge to do some serious windsurfing, get wet (and cooled off) kayaking, and try your hand at white-water rafting. And, of course, you can always enjoy a picnic—outside at a winery, in a meadow, on a riverbank or lakeshore, or on an outcropping. If you choose the latter, beware the rattlesnakes; they aren't very common, but they do turn up now and then.

There aren't any rattlers in Washington's other Wine Country, the one west of the Cascades—it's too cool and damp for them. The Salish Sea is a boating paradise where you can go cruising, fishing, and crabbing, or just hang out in a quiet cove and watch the water rise and fall with the tide. Here, too, you can ski, in season, within a couple of hours of the local wineries' tasting rooms.

■ STRONG FEELINGS ABOUT WINE

Washingtonians have strong feelings about wine, because making wine here has required a long and sometimes fierce struggle—a harder one, perhaps, than anywhere else in the United States. Though the state's wine history is nearly as long as that of California, Prohibition hit Washington's wine industry more severely than it did the Golden State's, and the revival of Washington winemaking had to wait until the domestic wine boom of the 1960s and 1970s. To their credit, Washington wine buffs have always supported their winemakers, even during the dark days when the wines were not all up to snuff; they understood that supporting Washington's winemakers meant investing in the future. Now, with Washington wines regularly ranked among the best in the world, this support is stronger than ever.

My first taste of Washington wines was in the early 1970s, when I still lived in California, and when there were only a handful of Washington wineries to choose from. Shortly afterward, when I moved to the Pacific Northwest, I began to seek out local wines, unaware the region's wineries were just beginning to establish themselves. I had trouble making sense of the highly variable quality; but a slim book titled *Winery Tours in Oregon, Washington, Idaho, & British Columbia,* by the *Seattle Times* columnist Tom Stockley, came to my rescue. Only 100 pages long, it listed fewer than 40 wineries for the entire region (some of them with dubious credentials), yet Stockley's effort marked the beginning of an exciting era in which new wineries sprang up with every vintage. There are now several hundred wineries in the Pacific Northwest—a dramatic increase since 1978, when Stockley wrote his seminal volume—although as I write only one new wine district, the Walla Walla Valley, has come to the fore.

Having lived in California at a time when its wines first achieved international acclaim, I was underwhelmed by Washington wines at first. They were pleasant enough—wines to be sipped on the back porch on a warm afternoon or enjoyed with friends while telling stories by the fire—but not wines to write home about. That quickly changed: the wines improved vintage by vintage. Consumers unused to appreciating good wines suddenly began talking about grape varieties and growing conditions, and they started to compare the virtues of Yakima Valley wines with those from the Puget Sound region. Because good wine was still inexpensive in those early days, wine lovers held many tastings to compare the best of Washington with the best of California and Europe. Washington soon began to hold its own.

Despite the occasional glitch, overall quality has so increased that the best wines made in Washington rank among the best produced anywhere in the world. New wineries and grape varieties bring surprises with every vintage. And as more and more visitors spend vacation time in the wine valleys, new restaurants and inns are opening their doors to cater to their needs. Best of all, much of Washington's Wine Country and many of its wines are still little known, making this a perfect region to explore.

Wine is a very complex product of art and nature. More than any other fruit, grapes owe their aromas, their flavors, and their overall qualities to the soil and climate in which they're raised. Different growing conditions produce significant variations, and no other state has as great a variety of viticultural settings. In Washington, perhaps more than anywhere else in the West, you need to travel to understand both vineyards and wineries. Tastings at the suburban wineries of the Puget Sound region, which is devoid of vines, are different from those at minuscule lowland and island wineries, surrounded by postage stamp–sized vineyards. A visit to one of the tiny wineries in the Yakima Valley, the Walla Walla Valley, or the Columbia Gorge, where winemakers and their spouses personally pour you sips and tell you about their family aspirations, is nothing like a pilgrimage to those often overwhelming temples to wine that large corporations have erected.

So get ready to travel with me—even if it's only from your armchair, with a glass of Washington wine to prepare you for the trip.

Merlot grapes drying in the morning light.

THE SETTING

AS A WINE-PRODUCING STATE, Washington is unique—not because it has more than one wine-producing area, but because its two major wine regions differ so radically from each other. Both regions receive enough warmth to ripen grapes, but not the same varieties of grapes.

The region west of the Cascade Mountains—the inlets, valleys, foothills, and mountains of western Washington—has a maritime climate, with cool summers and mild winters. Here growers cultivate cool-climate grapes, such as chardonnay, pinot noir, Riesling, and siegerrebe, even though summers may often be warmer than those of Europe's more northerly grape-growing regions, where these varieties were developed. The regions east of the Cascade Mountains—the foothills of the eastern Cascades, the Columbia Plateau, the Okanogan Highlands, the Rocky Mountains (which reach Washington State in the Selkirks, north of Spokane), the Palouse Hills, and the Blue Mountains of central and eastern Washington—have a continental climate. With their hot summers and cold winters, these areas would be too warm for growing high-quality wine grapes were their hot days not tempered by cool nights.

Threshing wheat at harvest time, near Waterville, 1907.

■ Puget Sound Lowlands

The Puget Sound Lowlands—west of the Cascade Mountains, north of Thurston County, and east of the Olympic Mountains—comprise the islands of Puget Sound, the San Juan Islands, and the lowlands and foothills between the Sound and the Cascades. A very beautiful region, it's overlooked by the snow-capped peaks of the northern Cascades and the Olympic Mountains and by the volcanic cones of Mount Baker and Mount Rainier. The dense forests of western red cedar, Douglas fir, and western hemlock that once dominated the landscape have given way to vegetable fields, berry patches, orchards—and cities. But the forests endure on the ridges towering above the fields and the cities, and they still dominate the hills and the mountains.

Great amounts of rain may fall here during the winter, but the summers are usually dry. And what occasional rains there are rarely disturb the grapes, because the vineyards are planted on exceptionally well-drained glacial moraines or alluvial gravels left behind by receding glaciers from the last ice age, about 10,000 years ago. Countless convoluted saltwater channels and inlets cut deeply into the land, carrying tidal waters far inland and exerting a moderating influence on the climate. Summers here are cool, but the long daylight hours allow cool-climate grapes to ripen fully. The grapes planted in this region have better acidity and produce crisper, more refreshing wines than those grown in the warm-climate vineyards east of the Cascades. Vineyards have sprung up on Bainbridge, Whidbey, Lopez, and San Juan Islands, as well in the valleys and on the low ridges bordering the Skagit River east of Anacortes and north of Mount Vernon in northwestern Washington's Nooksack Valley.

The handful of wineries in the Seattle area include several of Washington's largest producers, though they get their grapes from the Yakima and Columbia Valleys (and they often make their wines east of the mountains as well). These "vineyardless" wineries, many of them occupying scenic settings on the margins of towns and suburbs, are a consequence of demographics: the Puget Sound megalopolis has a population of cultured residents who appreciate wines and love visiting wineries but prefer to shop close to home. Because they also care about food and have fairly high incomes, they support not only wineries but restaurants too. This confluence of sophisticated urbanites, dedicated vintners, and creative chefs has led to a major culinary renaissance in the region during the past three decades.

■ SOUTHERN LOWLANDS

The Southern Lowlands, which stretch from southern Puget Sound to the Columbia River, have few wineries, even though this is prime grape-growing country, with well-drained alluvial soils and a warmer climate than that of the Puget Sound Lowlands. The Willapa Hills protect the region from cold air coming off the Pacific Ocean, and the southern Cascades shield it from the heat of the interior valleys. Though the area has its share of arctic blasts and periodic deep freezes, winters here can be quite mild. In many ways, the Southern Lowlands resemble Oregon's Willamette Valley, though the soils differ and summers in the lowlands are a touch cooler. The wines produced from local grapes tend to be bigger than those to the north, yet crisper than those of the Willamette Valley. Puget Sound wineries eagerly seek out the grapes grown here, especially pinot noir, chardonnay, and some pinot gris.

One winery, Salishan, has been been producing for nearly three decades; several new ventures have since joined it. But tourism has yet to blossom in the Southern Lowlands. There are few great inns and restaurants outside the cities of Olympia, to the north, and Vancouver (Washington), near the Oregon border—perhaps because most travelers tend to hurry through these lowlands on their way to Portland or Seattle, or while en route to the much more scenic Cascade Mountains, Columbia River, or outer coast.

■ COLUMBIA PLATEAU

The blue-sky region east of the Cascade Mountain barrier is dominated by the Columbia Plateau, an immense bowl of volcanic rock—some 175 miles across—that drops from a height of more than 2,600 feet at its northern edge to a depression only a few hundred feet above sea level at its southernmost point. (See the "Geology, Climate, Landscape" chapter for more information.) This is a super-region that includes all the central and eastern Washington regions we'll be discussing: the Columbia River Gorge, the Columbia Valley, the Yakima Valley, and the Walla Walla Valley. The Columbia Valley lies entirely within the Columbia Plateau region, but the plateau extends far beyond it.

The western half of this region lies in the rain shadow of the Cascade peaks. (Clouds from the east drop moisture as they rise to cross the Cascades, becoming lighter; in the rain shadow on the mountains' western side, they drop far less.) A

Boats in Eagle Harbor, near Bainbridge Island Vineyards and Winery.

dry steppe of sagebrush and bunch grasses, the northern part is called the Sagebrush Sea; the hills to the east, which stretch beyond the rain shadow, were once densely covered by short bunch grasses but are now planted with wheat, legumes, and grapevines.

Although generally warm, the Columbia Plateau region does have some "cold" vineyards where cool-climate Riesling, gewürztraminer, and chenin blanc thrive. But most of the vineyards here are warm enough to ripen to perfection cabernet franc, cabernet sauvignon, merlot, sangiovese, sauvignon blanc, semillon, syrah, and even zinfandel. Grapes were first planted in this region in the 1800s and then again in the 1930s, but viticulture did not take off until the wine boom of the 1960s and 1970s, when new areas were planted to vines and wineries began to sprout like mushrooms.

■ COLUMBIA RIVER GORGE

Though the vineyards, wineries, and wines of the Columbia River Gorge play only a minor role, relatively speaking, on the grand ecological level, they are one of the region's major attractions. The gorge is a truly spectacular place, cut by a river older than the mountains that stood in its way to the sea. Cliffs rising as high as 4,000 feet hem in the Columbia River and the small communities on its banks. Most of the vineyards lie on south-facing terraces high above the river, some looking toward Oregon's Mount Hood and invisible from below. Many wineries are right off highways and thus easy to reach. A pronounced climate change takes place from west to east within the Gorge, producing in turn a change in vegetation. The western cliffs are clad with the rainforest conifers of the western lowlands, but moving eastward the climate gradually changes until one sees, dominating the river, only the naked rock of dramatic cliffs, stripped bare of soil by the Spokane Floods and only sparsely dotted with sagebrush and grasses and an occasional oak or pine.

The Gorge can be reached from the Columbia and Walla Walla Valleys by way of the Tri-Cities (Richland, Kennewick, and Pasco), and from the western lowlands on scenic Route 14, which hugs the northern bank of the great river. Both the Washington and the Oregon banks have excellent amenities, originally developed for the well-to-do windsurfers who have flocked here for decades to brave the Gorge's fierce blows.

■ COLUMBIA VALLEY

The Columbia Valley is the largest of eastern Washington's wine regions, a vast American Viticultural Area (AVA), or appellation, that stretches from northern Oregon to Washington's Lake Chelan and Lake Roosevelt. It encompasses not only the bottomlands and slopes of the Columbia River, but the Yakima and Walla Walla Valleys, Red Mountain, and the eastern section of the Columbia River Gorge as well.

Most of the grapes in the Columbia Valley AVA are planted in the Pasco Basin, north of the Tri-Cities, and on slopes above the Snake River. Shielded from rain by the Cascade Mountains, this dry steppe was part of the Sagebrush Sea but is now largely given over to irrigated agriculture. Nevertheless, the Sagebrush Sea still brushes up against the fields, orchards, and vineyards, and laps at the margins of the valley's cities and farmlands. Unlike other Pacific Northwest wine regions, this is one where Concord grapes (a native American variety) have played as big a role in the past as the *Vitis vinifera* grapes from which most fine wines are made.

(above) Lake Chelan is one of the most beautiful destinations in the Columbia Valley.
(following pages) Backlit grapevines at Walla Walla's Seven Hills Vineyard. (Brent Bergherm)

The deep alluvial soils deposited by the Spokane Floods, which were temporarily dammed by the rocky cliffs of the Wallula Gap, make parts of the area quite flat, almost a plain. Basalt underlies these deposits, but although it's thick at the edges of the plateau, it's sunken toward the middle, creating a basinlike region. The Columbia River cuts through this region to the north, west, and south; the Snake River comes in from the east. Both have spectacular bluffs. Some parts of the landscape are truly odd—there's nothing quite like them anywhere else on earth. Basalt dikes rise above scabland channels, ponds, and lakes teeming with waterfowl. Marshes shelter shorebirds, yellow-headed and red-winged blackbirds, rails, muskrats, and beavers. Long-billed curlews, whose numbers declined when the steppe was plowed, have learned that there are bugs to be found in pastures and vineyards and that a cautious bird can successfully nest in a field. If you're lucky, you may see sandhill cranes, bald eagles, or white pelicans. Coyotes are everywhere: along the sides of roads, in broccoli fields, in vineyards. A few small patches of this region are true desert, inhabited by rattlesnakes, horned lizards, sage thrashers, and other such varmints. From late spring into summer, the slopes put on spectacular wildflower displays; in autumn, the creek and river bottoms are ablaze with the reds and golds of the season.

■ YAKIMA VALLEY

The Yakima Valley appellation encompasses the lower course of the Yakima River, a tributary of the Columbia, but, curiously, doesn't include the city of Yakima. It's separated from the rest of the Columbia Valley by the low ridge of Red Mountains west of the Tri-Cities, and from the Columbia River (which curls around it) to the north by the 3,000-foot-plus Rattlesnake Hills and to the south by the 2,000-foot-high Horse Heaven Hills; to the west, Ahtanum Ridge separates the valley from the city of Yakima and the Ahtanum Valley.

The serenely pastoral Yakima Valley is flanked by vineyard-covered slopes and grassy ridges and overtowered by the tall, snowcapped volcanic peaks of Mount Rainier and Mount Adams. The latter, which can be seen from most of the valley's higher slopes, is called *Pahto* by the members of the Yakama Nation and venerated as a spirit. The Yakima Valley is cooler than the Columbia Valley, and grapes grown here show an extra touch of refinement. Valley farms also produce a great variety of crops, including asparagus, hops, hot and sweet peppers, apples, apricots, cherries, melons, peaches, and plums.

This long valley, with its long ridges, also owes its deep alluvial soils to deposits made by the Spokane Floods. Besides tall sagebrush, these soils support grasses that look like soft fur when the wind ruffles them. Hawks, long-billed curlews, and coyotes can often be spotted, mountain goats are common on cliffs of the Cascades, and wild horses still roam the remote valleys and ridges of Horse Heaven Hills.

There are few cultural amenities outside the city of Yakima to the west and the Tri-Cities to the east. But the valley has a vibrant Hispanic culture, with small taquerias, cantinas, and mercados in every town and hamlet. Travelers looking for a quick snack can patronize the many "taco trucks" that dispense tasty tacos, made with hand-patted tortillas, filled with a variety of barbecued meats, and accompanied by freshly made salsa—but, alas, no wine.

■ RED MOUNTAIN

Between Prosser and Richland, the Yakima River makes a big bend to the north; the low ridge that rises in and above it is a recent appellation. Red Mountain's soils are among the most powdery, and thus the best drained, in the state, and although the mountain has some of the region's hottest weather, the nearby Yakima River assures a rapid nocturnal cooldown even at the height of summer—perfect conditions for creating the high sugars, high acids, and complex flavors that turn grapes into superior wines.

■ WALLA WALLA VALLEY

The Walla Walla Valley is a green jewel east of the Wallula Gap. Surrounded by rolling hills to the north and south and bordered by the conifer-clad Blue Mountains to the east, much of the valley lies beyond the rain shadow of the Cascade Mountains, allowing for successful agriculture (including grapegrowing) without irrigation. The valley's deep alluvial soils were, again, deposited by the Spokane Floods, but the hills are largely composed of loess—fine wind-blown dust, whose sharp-edged soil particles allow for quite steep slopes that can collapse catastrophically in very wet years. The tree-lined Touchet (pronounced "TOO-shee") and Walla Walla Rivers, filled with runoff from the Blue Mountains, traverse the valley. A scenic spur of the Blue Mountains protects the valley from most frigid winter winds; it's often warmer than Seattle in midwinter and has almost as long a growing season.

The Walla Walla Valley falls under the Columbia Valley appellation, but it also is an appellation itself, and during the 1990s it emerged as Washington's premier grape-growing and wine-making region. The city of Walla Walla has all of the accoutrements of a proper Wine Country town: wineries, comfortable inns, first-rate restaurants, shops, theaters, and an outstanding farmers' market.

■ A Complex Mosaic

The regions of Washington's Wine Country, unlike those of northern California's, differ markedly from those of southern France and northern Italy; nor do they have much in common with those of northern France, Germany, or elsewhere in Europe. Settled largely by puritanical farmers from the Midwestern Bible Belt and by dour Scandinavians, the eastern Washington Wine Country has always lacked the Mediterranean joie de vivre of the California Wine Country, though things are changing now. Western Washington, on the other hand, was settled by loggers, boat builders, and fishermen, many of them of Adriatic ancestry, who loved wine with their meals (and made their own when it couldn't be bought). These are the people who provided the spark that started Washington's modern wine industry. It's difficult to sum up these diverse regions in a few sentences, because they form such a complex geographic and cultural mosaic. But wine is a universal language, and during the past 30 years it has helped erase cultural differences—so Washington's "westsiders" are no longer surprised when they see a cowboy enjoying a glass of cabernet with a slab of steak.

(opposite) Cabernet grapes, vines, and sign at the Red Mountain's Hedges Vineyards.
(following pages) A man tends a row of Yakima Valley grapes in this 1912 photograph.

STEPPING INTO HISTORY

THE AUTUMN EVENING IS AS BALMY as the day was warm; there's not a cloud in sight that might signal the start of the rainy season in the San Juan Islands. From my perch high on Orcas Island's 2,409-foot Mount Constitution, I'm gazing out over a region of rock and saltwater inlets, forested ridges and snowcapped peaks—one of the world's most interesting wine regions. Far to the south, out of view, lies Stretch Island, where Washington's first commercial winery was established, in the 1870s. The snowy crags of the Cascade Mountains shield the wine-growing valleys of eastern Washington from the rains and cool air of the Pacific Ocean. Closer at hand, the Nooksack Valley to the northeast, the Skagit Valley to the southeast, Whidbey and Lopez Islands to the south, and San Juan Island to the west have their own vineyards and wineries. All but one of these wineries grow grapes, though they all supplement their harvests with grapes from eastern Washington vineyards. (A couple of them also produce wines from other local fruits.)

Even in West Coast terms, these wineries are quite new—the oldest was established little more than 20 years ago. This is true for most of Washington's other wineries as well, on both sides of the Cascade Mountains. The fact is that Washington's wine history doesn't go back very far, even though grapes were first planted north of the Columbia River in the 1820s by the gardeners at Fort Vancouver, the Hudson's Bay Company's major outpost in the Pacific Northwest.

Wine grapes are not indigenous to Washington. At Fort Vancouver, grapes were planted from grape seeds brought from England shortly after the fort's establishment; only later were they augmented with vines transported from Europe. These were most likely table grapes, not wine grapes. Records show that wine was served at Fort Vancouver only at formal meals, because John McLoughlin, the chief factor (as the commanding officer was known), was an almost complete teetotaler and discouraged the consumption of wine with daily meals. The fort had vineyards, but the grapes were probably not made into wine—though they were enjoyed as fresh fruit. Narcissa Whitman, a Protestant missionary who visited Fort Vancouver in 1836, wrote about plucking grapes from the arbor at the chief factor's house: "The grapes are just ripe and I am feasting on them finely."

There were other early plantings: by the Oblate padres (Catholic missionaries who were active during the early years of Pacific Northwest settlement) at their Yakima mission; by pioneer farmers in the Walla Walla Valley; and, as Ron Irvine attests in his excellent 1997 history of Washington winemaking, *The Wine Project,* by at least one homesteader in the Ahtanum Valley, near Tampico, west of Yakima. Irvine describes viewing early vines that have survived for more than a century.

Bicyclists pass a historic church in the San Juan Islands.

Grapes were also planted during the latter half of the 19th century near Moxee, Wenatchee, and Lake Chelan, areas that for the past hundred years have produced mainly apples. Some of these orchards were pulled up and replaced, not by the traditional vinifera grapes of Europe—which had gotten the California wine industry off to a healthy start, and had inspired commercial winemaking in Washington— but rather by native American grapes, which grew well and ripened satisfactorily in the state's diverse climes but produced inferior wine. The Island Belle, a Midwestern variety also known as Campbell Early, yielded a high-alcohol wine of little refinement—just the stuff to satisfy loggers and fishermen. A few of these vines survive on islands in southern Puget Sound and their grapes are still being made into wine by one winery there, Hoodsport.

Though Washington's first successful commercial vineyard and winery were established on Stretch Island, in southern Puget Sound, it was inevitable that vinifera grapes, as well as native American varieties, should eventually make their way east of the Cascade Mountains, where other fruit plantings thrived after irrigation became readily available at the beginning of the 20th century. Yet, aside from some sporadic post-Prohibition endeavors, there were no widespread plantings of wine grapes in the region until the past few decades. However, grapegrowers are

making up for lost time, and there are now vineyards from the Yakima River Canyon to the foothills of the Blue Mountains, and from the Columbia River Gorge to Lake Chelan. Growers are also developing other regions of Washington, and it looks like the coming decades will bring some exciting enological changes.

■ A PATCHY HISTORY

Like grapegrowing, winemaking in Washington has a patchy history. Most of what we know is anecdotal—fascinating tales that can't always be fully verified. But, as pioneer vintners and gardeners understood, the soil and the climate of this region were perfect for growing grapes. The soils were lean and well-drained, just the way vines like it. The climate was mild, with warm days and cool nights (to put good fruit flavor and acid into the grapes), and rainfall was ample. This was a land where a budding vintner could stick vine cuttings into the ground and, with minimal care, watch them produce superior grapes.

And that's exactly what the earliest vintners did. Old-world winemakers who had migrated to Washington fashioned excellent wines from these grapes, and immigrant coopers made vats and barrels for aging and fermenting them—and yet, after some initial accolades, the Washington wine industry languished, for reasons more cultural than agricultural. While French-Canadian trappers and European immigrants were used to enjoying wine with their meals, the Midwestern farmers and Scandinavian loggers who made up the bulk of the early settlers were not. They preferred beer and whiskey, and if they drank wine at all it had to be strong stuff. Such wine could be made as easily (and less expensively) from the fruit of highly productive apple trees and berry vines. The Adriatic fishermen who arrived later found such wines unappealing and preferred to make their own, often from grapes shipped north from California by train. Perhaps it was the ease with which they could get California grapes that kept these home winemakers from clamoring for local vineyards. Why risk making wine from grapes of unknown quality when you had such easy access to inexpensive high-quality grapes?

How differently would Europe's wine industries—most notably that of France—have evolved if they'd been established *after* railroads made it easy to ship grapes from one region to another? It's conceivable that the French would have

(top) A mildly psychedelic Spinner apple label from the 1930s and 1940s. (bottom) A pensive Uncle Sam touts his namesake brand in this 1920s and 1930s label.

developed very different attitudes toward grapes and toward the way wines are made. France's great wineries might now be in Paris, instead of in the provincial cities of Beaune and Bordeaux. And the British, instead of buying French claret, might have preferred to buy the grapes and make their own. This is all idle speculation, but there's no question that high-speed transportation made it possible during Prohibition for home winemakers in, say, Chicago and New York to make passable wines from California grapes. Modern transport by rail also explains the quirkiness of Washington's wine industry, with several of its largest wineries successfully established in the Seattle metropolitan area, close to the center of the state's population, but far from its vineyards.

■ Home Winemaking

If the growing of wine grapes and the art of winemaking didn't fully catch on in Washington until recently, neither did they ever fully vanish. A few wineries hung on, producing mainly for Washingtonians of German, French, Italian, and Slavic ancestry, and providing a source of grapes for those who wished to make their own. Wherever central and southern Europeans settled, they made wine to accompany their meals. Washington was no exception. And if traditional European wine grapes weren't always available, these wine lovers were willing to experiment with any fermentable fruits: apples, berries, even native American table grapes brought west by enterprising gardeners (since grapes aren't native to Washington). Wine grapes, vineyards, and a few wineries survived Prohibition, but what little demand there was for good wine was easily satisfied by imports from Europe and California and by home winemaking.

Except for a handful of commercial wineries that made mostly fortified fruit wines, Washington winemaking remained largely a home affair from Prohibition until the wine boom of the 1970s, when commercial winemaking spread north from California, first to Oregon and then to Washington. Even then, however, home winemaking played an important role, since several of the state's most successful commercial wineries got their impetus from their owners' or winemakers' successes with homemade wines. Home winemaking kept alive the means and the skills to bring about a wine revolution when the time was right. It's still popular even now.

Though many home winemakers in the Northwest used grapes shipped north from California, some also used locally grown grapes (thus helping to keep some of the older vineyards viable). In his 1948 book *The Unprejudiced Palate,* the late

Waitsburg, in Walla Walla County, photographed in 1876.

wine and food guru Angelo Pellegrini, a University of Washington professor and renowned home winemaker, wrote about a vineyard planted in the late 1800s:

> The finest wine I have ever made in America I am obliged to attribute, indirectly and ironically, to a young village schoolmistress whom I met in one of my classes several years ago. For it was she who gave me the name of W. H. Myers Jr., a vineyardist in The Dalles, Oregon, on the Columbia River, a little known but excellent wine grape district. This distinguished and obliging viticulturalist has been supplying me, during the past several years, with half a ton of muscats every October. The vineyard is about sixty years old, comprises but a few acres, and is ideally situated on the rolling hills which rise off the south bank of the river. The vines are exposed to the summer sun throughout the day. Mr. Myers cuts them for me when they are thoroughly ripe and ships them so that I may crush them within thirty-six hours after they leave the vineyard. The wine is excellent by the most exacting standards.

But, like other Northwest home winemakers, Pellegrini bought the bulk of his grapes, primarily zinfandel and alicante, from California vineyards. I once tasted one of his reds and did indeed find it excellent.

The Zillah Band marches in the 1913 Apple Blossom Festival.

■ DELAYED REACTION

Why did the switch from home to commercial winemaking in Washington take so long? One reason may be that the state lacked creative entrepreneurs like the McCreas, of Stony Hill Vineyard, and the Davies, of Schramsberg Vineyards, who helped raise the level of California wines to new heights. Nor did Washington have well established "wine dynasties," like California's Gallos, Martinis, Mondavis, and Pedroncellis. Another problem, mentioned by the few who tasted early Washington wines and passed on their comments, was that these wines weren't very good, and Washingtonians, who had honed their palates on the best wines Europe and California had to offer, saw little reason to drink them. Commenting candidly on this awkward period in the history of Northwest winemaking, the former *Seattle Times* wine columnist Tom Stockley has written, "There was a time, in the not-so-distant past, when wines of the Pacific Northwest were, to put it mildly, laughable."

Two post-Prohibition developments also hampered the industry: liquor laws and taxes made it difficult to sell good wine at reasonable prices; and the lure of native American Concord grapes, which ripened to perfection in the Columbia Basin, created a huge demand for these grapes among makers of canned and frozen grape juice and among California and New York wineries, which used them for their inexpensive fortified and "pop" wines. Little wonder that there was such a delay among Washingtonians in establishing wineries—they were given little hope that locally made wines would be taken seriously by connoisseurs.

■ TIMES CHANGE—AND THE WINES

The restrictive laws and taxes were softened in the 1970s, and the monopolistic (and provincial) state liquor board's stranglehold on the industry eased just in time for the domestic wine boom to engulf the Northwest and to enrich the region with new vineyards, new grape varieties, and new wineries. Best of all, a new crop of university-educated (and California-trained) winemakers, who knew what they were doing, began creating world-class wines right from the start.

Today, about 75 percent of Washington State wines are produced by two national conglomerates: U.S. Tobacco's Stimson Lane (Chateau Ste. Michelle, Columbia Crest, Farron Ridge, Snoqualmie, North Star, et al.) and Canandaigua's Columbia (Columbia, Covey Run, Paul Thomas). You don't even have to leave the Seattle metro area to visit the modern tasting rooms of these wineries, because you can do

(top) This 1884 photograph depicts the first house built in Sedro, Skagit County.
(bottom) Moxee Avenue, Moxee City, in 1918.

so at their corporate headquarters in Woodinville—they're across the street from each other. Though they're worth a visit to acquaint yourself with winemaking on a large scale, you don't have to visit the tasting rooms to find the wines—they're sold in just about every supermarket in Washington and throughout the West.

But small family wineries also thrive in Washington, in the Puget Sound region, and in the Columbia, Yakima, and Walla Walla Valleys. Each has its own unique history, which we'll touch upon as we visit. These wineries are especially worth a pilgrimage, because their wines are often available only there—and because their proprietors have such fascinating stories to tell.

TK

FOOD AND WINE

RED ROCKFISH, PURPLE OCTOPI, SILVER SALMON, pearly squid, blue mussels, gray-shelled oysters (with bits of seaweed attached), and orange Dungeness crabs are piled high on crushed ice, next to a stand where tidy rows of tomatoes, zucchini, cabbages, white and yellow sweet corn, lavender eggplants, various herbs, green and red apples, and golden peaches are arranged with artistic flair. There's food as far as the eye can see, in stalls and on tables that line one long, covered arcade, and in open-fronted shops along Pike Place, the cobbled street that gives the **Pike Place Market** its name.

It's a sight visitors to Seattle know well. Many of them have eaten at the intimate cafés whose tall windows overlook the Sound; on sunny restaurant decks or patios, they've dined on local seafood and sipped local wines. And they've done so in the company of Seattle residents, for the Pike Place Market is far more than a tourist attraction. It's one of the best food markets in the country, with the pick of the best food available in the city and the state. From the high bluffs on which the market sprawls, the eye wanders to **Elliott Bay,** which connects to Puget Sound and other inland waters, the source of much of the state's fresh seafood; and to snow-covered peaks, on whose sunny lower slopes some of Washington's best fruits and vegetables are grown. Wine shops anchor Pike Place at both its northern and southern ends. The minuscule Market Cellar Winery, tucked into its lower reaches, makes wine from Columbia Valley grapes.

More important than the Market's appeal to visitors is its role in purveying locally produced seasonal foods. They're usually available at the Market first, because this is where the growers bring them as soon as they're ready for harvest. If you're looking for arugula, beets, baby bok choy, celeriac, chive blossoms, cilantro, dandelion greens, organic horseradish roots, kohlrabi, komatsuna ("mustard spinach"), mizuna, red and green mustard greens, pea shoots, peppercress, purple asparagus, radishes (black, red, and white), rapini, rhubarb, Siberian kale, sorrel, sugar snap peas, Swiss chard (white, red, rainbow), sweet Walla Walla onions, spring garlic with green tops, mint, parsley, tarragon, sage, thyme—this is the place. Here's where you get the summer's first fresh berries and tomatoes, and the best and freshest of seafoods, from Kumamoto oysters to Manila clams and geoduck. You can also find an assortment of eggs, from free-range chicken and Araucana hens, from ducks, geese, and quail; a rich variety of cheeses (some extremely hard to find elsewhere); and dozens of sausages.

Pike Place Market is one of the best food markets in the country, a place where you're guaranteed to find the freshest purple octopi and pearly squid, along with superb produce.

If you don't feel like cooking in your hotel room, you can stock up on prepared foods, from roasted game hen and sake teriyaki beef to chicken skewers, sweet-and-sour cabbage-and-apple salad, and, of course, any number of delectable sandwiches. And you can buy a bottle of Washington wine to accompany your meal at **DeLaurenti's Specialty Food and Wine** or the **Pike and Western Wine Shop.**

The Pike Place Market represents the quintessence of the local culinary experience, but it hardly stands alone. It serves as an inspiration for the state's farmers' markets, the best of which operate in Olympia, Pasco, and Walla Walla. And its very presence motivates Seattle supermarkets to stock up on fresh local foods to stay competitive. These Seattle supermarkets have, in turn, inspired the ones in smaller towns, to the point that there's now an excellent selection of seasonal foods in markets throughout the state.

Washingtonians love to picnic—in the mountains, on river banks, on the beach, in boats. The meal you bring along can be as simple as a loaf of bread and a bottle of wine. Or you might stop at an oyster farm for fresh oysters and—since the farms sell more than just oysters—freshly cooked Dungeness crab. You could gather wild oysters, mussels, or clams at the beach, or catch crabs at low tide. Bring a kettle, and you can boil or steam your catch on the spot. Fire the coals at a picnic-area grill and spread clams, mussels, and oysters over them.

Your picnic could include a wide variety of smoked foods—clams, salmon, oysters, sturgeon, mussels—or perhaps pickled salmon, a smoked-salmon potato salad, or a cold clam pie. Don't pass up the small-town bakeries as you travel—let yourself be drawn in by the heady aromas of oven-fresh breads, pastries, and cookies. If the time of year is right, you'll find apple cider, freshly pressed—the kind your grandparents (or somebody's)

Washington's bounty includes Pasco produce.

Washingtonians love to picnic—in the mountains, on river banks, in boats, and on beaches.

made on the family farm. Keep your eyes open for unexpected finds: tasty beef jerky, smoked sausages, a new variety of apples, or a new style of meltingly tender smoked oysters. You may discover a new grower of succulent vegetables, a new cheese maker, a newly opened winery. Even established wineries often have one or two wines sold only on the premises. As you travel in Washington Wine Country, tuck a well-chilled ice chest into the trunk of your car to make sure any provisions you buy on the road won't spoil between stops—an important precaution, because you're likely to acquire more than you can eat.

During the past two decades, an increasing number of Americans and foreign travelers have come to Washington to enjoy its unparalleled scenic beauty, and because these visitors enjoy the state's superb foods and wines, they help spread the word. In a 1984 visit to Seattle, the French wine expert Armand Cottin praised the quality of our foods, past and present, observing that we'd always had the greatest of raw materials available to us and we were learning how to use them "properly." At the dawn of the new millennium, we're no longer just "learning." We can proudly point to our foods, and to the dishes prepared by our chefs, as some of the world's best. And now we can point with the same pride to our wines.

■ LOCAL FOODS MAKE GOOD (MEALS)

To better highlight Washington's foods, let's take a quick look at which local foods take on special qualities here. Among the state's excellent cheeses are the cow's- and goat's-milk cheeses made by Quillisascut, east of Lake Roosevelt, and the nutty, richly flavored goudas that Pleasant Valley Dairy and Samish Bay Cheese create near the shores of the Salish Sea. Goat cheeses of the soft chèvre varieties also abound, but their producers face periodic mold problems and rarely stay in business for more than a couple of years. But keep your eyes open—somehow, new producers always seem to crop up. The state's largest cheese producer is the giant Darigold plant near Sunnyside, which cranks out more than 400,000 pounds of cheddar-style cheese *every day.*

Fish and shellfish are plentiful, from local waters and Alaska's. (Much of Alaska's fishing fleet is based in Washington ports.) Though salmon are not as common as they once were, both fresh and smoked salmon are still in plentiful supply. Look

With clams, oysters, mussels, squid, and octopi, Pike Place Market is shellfish heaven. The market has raised awareness of locally grown and harvested foods so much that it has inspired farmers' markets and even supermarkets to stock better and fresher foods.

for the best specimens in small local smokehouses, in fishing-port towns such as Bellingham, Ilwaco, Seattle, and Westport. In the ocean ports, you can also find excellent fresh (in season) albacore and smoked albacore, as well as fresh and smoked halibut. Oysters and scallops also come fresh and smoked. Another fish that's delectable when smoked is the richly flavored, almost oily sablefish (most commonly sold as black cod, though it's not even distantly related to the cods). "Rock cod" is actually local rockfish, often sold as red snapper, which it's not, though it's good in its own right. At Chinese restaurants and at some upscale Seattle restaurants (most notably **Flying Fish**), you can order it cooked whole. True cod is most commonly served up as fish and chips; so is lingcod, which, once again, is not a cod but a greenling—that is, a type of kelp fish. Other regional seafood highlights include flounder (most commonly touted as sole or English sole in both restaurants and seafood markets), smelt, sturgeon, and trout. All are delicious, and all go very well with a dry Northwest Riesling, chenin blanc, sémillon, and sauvignon blanc. Some Washingtonians prefer to accompany salmon and albacore with Oregon pinot noir or Washington merlot.

Washington is famous for its oysters; the state is now the largest producer of oysters in North America, if not the world. Oyster season usually runs from September through April, when oysters are raised in shallow bays. They come in several varieties, including the tiny native Olympia, the slightly larger Kumamoto, the Pacific oyster (which comes in a variety of sizes, from half-dollar to steak). The state is also renowned for its flavorful razor clams. They're available at odd times and may be dug only by sport fishermen. Other clams, however, are usually plentiful, including small steamers and giant geoducks, which are among the largest clams in the world. All of them are quite tender and have a delicate flavor. Scallops are common in the waters of the Salish Sea and are usually served in their shells and eaten whole, like steamed clams. The best blue mussels are farmed in Penn Cove and in other protected inlets of the region. Washingtonians accompany oysters and clams with a crisp sémillon or sauvignon blanc, although some swear they taste better with Riesling, pinot gris, or even pinot noir.

Dungeness crab abounds in offshore waters and in the sheltered inlets of the Salish Sea, and is either caught commercially or trapped by sport fishermen. The delicate, sweet meat is nicely enhanced by chenin blanc and Riesling. Other tasty regional crustaceans include the tiny bay shrimp as well as spot prawns, which can grow quite large; look for signs at roadside stands, which often sell the freshest

Early-20th-century fishermen brailing salmon from a fish trap in the Puget Sound area.

shrimp. Shrimp and prawns, as well as the small crayfish of lakes and rivers, go especially well with the crisp white wines produced in the Puget Sound region.

Beef raised in Washington's dryland pastures is exceptional. The choicest comes from local farmers, who usually sell the meat straight off the farm. The same is true of lamb, the best of which comes from the San Juan Islands. Oddly, Washington raises very little of that great American staple, pork. While this quirk doesn't translate into a shortage of bacon, don't be surprised if the omelet you order at a coastal diner comes with smoked salmon instead. There's also excellent chicken (ideally paired with chardonnay or Riesling) as well as duck (with pinot noir or merlot). Rabbit and farm-raised quail are also high-quality. The state abounds in venison (deer and elk) and game birds (wild ducks and geese, grouse, band-tailed pigeons, valley quail, chukar partridge, and even wild turkey), but those meats are rarely available to visitors. If, however, you're lucky enough to be invited to a venison dinner, bring a bottle of Yakima Valley cabernet sauvignon, Walla Walla Valley merlot, or Columbia Valley syrah.

Washington restaurants pride themselves on serving the best and freshest of local vegetables—tiny "new" Yukon Gold or red potatoes, broccoli, cauliflower, sweet and sugar snap peas, green beans, and—east of the Cascades—sweet corn, sweet onions, vine-ripened tomatoes, and full-flavored hot and mild chili peppers. The Yakima and Walla Walla Valleys are famous for their tender, exceptionally flavorful asparagus, in green and purple varieties, although now and then a grower takes extra pains to raise white asparagus. Globe artichokes are raised commercially on the Olympic Peninsula, in the Skagit Valley, and on Vashon Island. Washington beets and leeks are so flavorful they're in a class by themselves. Restaurants also serve wild vegetables (gathered by professional collectors), including various kelps (often served as "ocean salad"), pickleweed and other wild greens, and a wide variety of wild mushrooms. Washington is famous, too, for its apples, apricots, cherries, nectarines, peaches, raspberries, and strawberries. The state also produces hazelnuts and sweet, succulent melons. Many of these vegetables and fruits go well with local wines: asparagus and artichokes with sémillon and sauvignon blanc; wild mushrooms with Northwest reds; and kelp, surprisingly, with chardonnay. A touch of Riesling improves apples, melons, peaches, pears, and strawberries; muscat does marvels for apricots and berries. Cherries go unexpectedly well with pinot noir.

Washington restaurants pride themselves on serving the freshest local vegetables—broccoli, snap peas, green beans, beets, leeks, and "wild" vegatables that include kelp and pickleweed

■ DINING OUT

Washington's bounty is reflected in the dishes served at its restaurants, where brave chefs may match up seemingly incongruous foods and wines. In the spring of 2003, for example, when the elegant **Ponti Seafood Grill** held its annual celebration of the first Copper River salmon to arrive from Alaska, its kitchen paired the fish not only with local sauvignon blanc but also with cabernet sauvignon and red Bordeaux blends. These matches worked splendidly. So did the partnering of Dungeness crab and cabernet. Washington red wines also work well with Asian flavors. No one has pushed this fusion cuisine as far as Ponti, with its unabashed Asian renderings of Northwest seafood dishes: grilled wild king salmon basted with olive oil, lime juice, soy sauce, fresh ginger, and cilantro; or Dungeness crab spring rolls with a chile-and-lime dipping sauce. No wonder many critics consider Ponti Seattle's finest seafood restaurant. With similar daring, Bruce Hiebert of Dayton's **Patit Creek Restaurant** has successfully matched a big Yakima Valley Riesling with beef. So, wherever you dine, don't be shy about ordering red wine with seafood or white wine with red meat. You might be pleasantly surprised.

In Washington, few restaurant menus are without one or two favorite oyster dishes.

Most seafood restaurants are more traditional than Ponti. **Ray's Boathouse,** on Shilshole Bay, has served a layered seafood terrine of shrimp, salmon, and scallops; a fragrant dish of linguine with baby clams in lemon-garlic and butter sauce; and grilled Alaska coho salmon fillet basted with herbed garlic butter, for which the wine steward recommends chardonnay or sauvignon blanc. Tradition merges with innovation. In Seaview, on the coast, the **42nd Street Café** serves local oysters fresh, on the half shell, but also pan-fried with Cajun mayonnaise. Fried razor clams come with a parsley-caper mayonnaise; locally caught chinook salmon might have a smoked sweet-pepper glaze; a pork chop might be flavored with a smoked cranberry barbecue sauce. You'd do well to accompany those dishes with chenin blanc from L'Ecole No. 41 in Walla Walla, a Yakima Valley sémillon from Chinook, or a Woodward Canyon Columbia Valley merlot. At a dinner prepared a few years ago at New York City's James Beard House, the chef from Kirkland's **Yarrow Bay Grill** dished up an octopus salad and a smoked-pheasant salad, wild king salmon in a pinot-noir sauce, morel and parsnip ravioli, and sweetbreads.

Dining choices in the cattle country east of the Cascades are no longer limited to steak, prime rib, and lamb chops. In Yakima, **Gasperetti's Gourmet Restaurant** has served such delights as smoked-salmon "cheesecake" with sauce verde and toast thins, and fresh Dungeness crabmeat cannelloni Florentine. In Spokane, **Milford's Fish House and Oyster Bar,** which specializes in fresh seafood, has offered its visitors Oregon bay shrimp quesadillas and fresh sea scallops with Walla Walla onions, pesto sauce, and cheese.

And which wines do these restaurants recommend with their dishes? As you may have already guessed, Washington diners have eclectic tastes and may insist on white wine with meat and red wine with seafood. Others stick to a wine of their choice—red or white—through all the courses of a lengthy meal. But over the years a few matches made in heaven have emerged: pinot noir, pinot gris, or sauvignon blanc with salmon; merlot or syrah with lamb; cabernet sauvignon and beef; Riesling and chicken; sémillon or sauvignon blanc with oysters, clams, or mussels; Riesling with Dungeness crab. Some chefs recommend local sparkling wines with salmon and pinot noir with oysters, rabbit, and scallops.

For more information about the restaurants mentioned in this chapter and about others in Washington State, see the Restaurants section of the "Practical Information" chapter.

■ COOKING WITH WINE

In Washington, cooking with wine is a predictably eclectic affair. While traditionalists may prepare seafood and chicken in white wine and red meat in red wine, I've tasted an excellent lamb dish cooked in a big, overblown chardonnay, oysters and mussels beautifully steamed in pinot noir, and delectable salmon poached in merlot. The acid level and flavor of the wine—as well as the chef's preference—is far more important in Northwest cookery than a wine's color.

This inclination stems in part from an attitude rooted in local eating habits. The cooking style of the Pacific Northwest's first settlers was informed by the region's bounty—because that was more or less all they had to eat. Fortunately, nature provided lots of good things: saltwater inlets and bays yielded crab and shrimp; rocks and pilings offered up mussels; tide flats exposed clams and oysters. As an old saying has it, "The table is set when the tide is out." (One congressman went on record with the remark "My constituents' stomachs rise and fall with the tide.")

Pioneer cookery in Washington was simple, relying mostly on the smoking, pickling, and boiling of fish and shellfish, as well as on home-baked breads and pies, both sweet and savory, filled with apples and huckleberries, or clams and oysters. The settlers had easy access to halibut, kelp fish, rockfish, and salmon, and from Native Americans they adopted a unique hard—that is, hot—smoking style still popular in the region. They learned to season their meals with wild vegetables, berries, and mushrooms. What little wine they had was homemade. Red-currant wine and apple cider were favorites.

Herbfarm serves up distinctive squab.

Salmon, the traditional staple of the coastal Northwest, was also important in the wheat and cattle country east of the Cascades, because salmon ascended the Columbia and Snake Rivers in great quantities until

The table is set for pleasure at Vintner's Inn.

the mid-1930s, when hydroelectric dams cut off their flow. These barriers didn't affect native trout: even now, the best trout streams are east of the Cascades.

Washington's cookery was reinvigorated in the 1970s and 1980s, when locally produced wines became widely available. At first the new wine styles were French-influenced, because the then-popular French restaurants (Seattle's Mirabeau, The Other Place, and Le Tastevin, all now defunct) experimented with the new wines. However, trained chefs were scarce and expensive, so winemakers' wives and winery staffers were drafted into the kitchen. Happily, they wound up leading the vanguard, imaginatively pairing local foods and wines and advancing the art of cooking with local wines.

Chefs in city and country restaurants took note. Northwest foods and wines soon became the rage. At first, chefs applied tried-and-true European methods to local wines and foods, but the best chefs were also the most creative, and a new exuberance percolated through the region's kitchens.

The trend continues, though even today restaurants that describe their fare as Northwestern often offer only a few regional dishes. On the other hand, Italian, French, and plain old American restaurants frequently perfect one or more notable

Northwestern preparations: smoked-salmon fettuccine (or smoked-salmon omelets or hash), salmon chowder, crab stew, oyster chowder, barbecued oysters, and smoked-oyster pizza. Such dishes are thoroughly Northwestern, though they appear in different guises—usually behind whatever fancy foreign names reflect the current culinary fad.

Why do Pacific Northwest wines lend themselves so well to cooking almost anything? One reason is their high level of natural acids. This acidity makes them ideal for reduction sauces, because it deepens the flavors of any foods cooked in the wines. Reduction also enhances their high level of fruit, adding unexpected nuances to a dish—as does the varietal flavor of the grape, which tends to be more pronounced in the Northwest than in warmer growing regions. There are few fancy touches. The berries and other wild fruits used by the earliest settlers found their way into the fish, meat, wine, and fruit cookery of Seattle's Sephardic food vendors early in the 20th century. These merchants wielded their influence mainly via Seattle's Pike Place Market, and they're responsible for such wonderful creations as salmon cooked with plums and lamb stewed in lemberger with raspberry puree.

Washington's cookery, like its wine, is still evolving. California is often thought of as America's Provence or Tuscany, because of its big, powerful wines and the hearty Mediterranean style of its restaurants. If we were to make a similar comparison, we could call the Pacific Northwest America's Alsace and Burgundy; the Northwest's "Mediterranean" dishes exhibit a greater affinity with the more delicate dishes of northeastern and north-central France than with the more robust fare of southern France and Italy and, for that matter, California. But what's true now may soon change. Only time will tell.

The land and weather work in tandem in Washington to produce strong grapes with uncommon variety, texture, and complexity. (Brent Bergherm)

GEOLOGY · CLIMATE
LANDSCAPE

Merlot grapes soak up the sun.

BENEATH GENTLE RIDGES SILVERED WITH SAGEBRUSH and weathered grasses, the valley stretches far to the west where, on the horizon, a range of snow-capped mountains closes the prospect. Two volcanic peaks tower above the lesser mountains and hills. Below the bluff, a river meanders across the valley floor, its course marked by the golden fall foliage of cottonwoods and willows. Above the pastures and cornfields that border the river, the slopes are covered with orchards, vineyards, and an occasional pumpkin patch. The soil that supports all this growth is soft and friable—almost sandy, and so light it swirls up wherever the wind disturbs it. Here and there, run-off water has cut deep gullies, exposing layers of soil remarkably uniform in color and texture. An occasional outcropping of black rock above the gently sloping ground adds contrast and a note of menace.

The clues to this landscape's origin lie in the soft soil and the black rock. Both are products of floods—the rock laid down millions of years ago in vast lava floods, the soil deposited 12,000 years ago by unstoppable floodwaters, released when a glacial lake in what is now western Montana burst its icy confines.

Both floods were so huge and moved so fast that they obliterated everything in their path. The glacier that dammed the river, creating the lake that was the source of the deluge, was one of many that covered Canada and parts of the northern United States during the last ice age, which lasted until some 10,000 years ago. East of the Cascades, the ice barely reached the edge of the Columbia Plateau, but it was thick enough to divert the Columbia River through the Grand Coulee. West of the Cascades, a glacial lobe covered the lowlands and scoured the inlets and channels that are now Puget Sound and the Salish Sea. After the ice receded, saltwater intruded from the ocean, filled the channels, and created islands, peninsulas, and headlands of various shapes and configurations. Landlocked depressions carved by the glacier became lakes.

All this water has significant effects on Washington's climate, making for cool summers and mild winters. The valleys, plateaus, and hills of eastern Washington are dry because rain clouds moving in from the Pacific drop their loads of water as they run into the Cascade Mountains. This pattern not only makes the western part of the state very wet but also results in runoff and erosion, adding alluvial deposits to the clays and gravels left behind by the continental glacier.

But eastern Washington isn't as dry as it seems because three large rivers—the Columbia, the Snake, and the Yakima—traverse the dry lands, making irrigation possible. These rivers provide the proof that almost anything connected with the geology of Washington is weird: already present when lava flows created the Columbia Plateau, they cut their way down through the mountains as their beds were elevated by tectonic forces, in the process preserving even some of the meanders created during their lowland incarnations.

By dividing what is now Washington State into two diverse regions, the natural forces of distant and recent geologic activity have given us two wine-growing regions that differ in structure and climate. But there are similarities as well. Both regions have mild climates—even eastern Washington receives some cooling marine influence. And both have the well-drained soils that are essential for successful viticulture. While the east gets warm enough in summer to ripen such warm-climate grapes as cabernet sauvignon and syrah, the west can ripen cool-climate grapes and may even be suited for chardonnay and pinot noir in its warmer parts.

Grapevines must be stressed to give their best; their fruit becomes the most complex when they're grown in well-drained soils and get little water. Many parts

An escarpment of the Columbia River Gorge. The gorge was shaped by a combination of fire and ice.

divergence in the quality of their wines. Yet this variety in growing conditions is what makes the wines of Washington so exciting.

It's strange that the modern vintner's art is so dependent on the forces of fire and ice that shaped this landscape in aeons past. The fire came first, some 15 million years ago, through the heat of friction as oceanic and continental plates pushed against each other. The pressures of these collisions created complex upliftings and foldings—making mountaintops out of ocean floors, crumbling tall peaks into the sea. The friction also created geologic hot spots that spewed lava aboveground. Outflows of what is now known as Columbia Basin basalt covered vast tracts of land east of the Cascades; surplus lava flowed out through the Columbia River Gorge all the way to the Oregon Coast, where it hardened and can still be seen in the form of prominent capes. The heavy lava depressed the land, and because it cooled more rapidly at its margins than in the middle, the plateau has a noticeable depression in its center. That's why this region is described as both a plateau and a basin. Today the basin's rim rises as much as 2,700 feet above sea level, while the elevation at its lowest point, at Wallula Gap, is only about 200 feet.

The ice came much later, long after the lava had solidified into basalt. At the time of the last great ice age, enormous ice lobes pushed south from Canada into what is now Washington State and also flowed down from the peaks of the Rockies and the Cascades into the valleys. Coastal British Columbia and Washington (as far south as the site of present-day Olympia) were buried under an ice sheet more than 3,500 feet thick. In the Puget Sound region, the Vashon Stade—the last of the continental glaciers covering the coast—melted between 13,500 and 11,500 years ago. East of the Cascades, the ice blocked the flow of the Columbia River, diverting its waters south through the Grand Coulee.

The ice blocked Montana's Clark's Fork as well, near the modern city of Missoula, forming a vast lake (known to geologists as Lake Missoula). But the ice dam holding back the lake proved to be unstable. It broke, refroze, and broke again over several millennia, each time sending a gargantuan flood toward the sea. The last of these floods occurred around 12,000 years ago, after human beings had already settled the region.

Probably no other part of the world has experienced floods as tremendous as the ones that ravaged the Columbia Plateau and the Columbia River Gorge. (These giant floods are finally getting the recognition they deserve: the U.S. Government is in the process of establishing a Spokane Floods National Park, with visitors centers in Washington's Yakima Valley and Oregon's Willamette Valley.) The Columbia riverbed proved too small to hold such a huge volume, and the rushing waters spilled over the southern rim of its canyon to carve multiple channels—of which the Grand Coulee and Moses Coulee are the largest—on its course to the Wallula Gap (near the modern-day Tri-Cities).

Massive lava flows and mighty river waters shaped the geography of the Columbia Plateau.

Once the floodwaters squeezed through the Wallula Gap, the raging torrents, still turbid with sediments, scoured rocks, soil, and vegetation from the walls of the Columbia Gorge, and, slowed by the narrowing of the riverbed near Rainier, surged up the Willamette Valley.

As the floods roared across the land, they tore out rocks and ground them down into boulders, cobbles, gravels, sands, and silts. The waters became turbid with debris. Wherever the floodwaters were slowed or even temporarily halted, the debris dropped from the water and settled as alluvial deposits. Most eastern Washington vineyards are planted on these deposits, which now form deep, quickly draining, similar soils throughout the Yakima, Columbia, and Walla Walla Valleys. Since the floodwaters were deep, the alluvial deposits range far up the valleys, in some places covering even hills. At Canoe Ridge, in the Horse Heaven Hills, they manifest themselves as loose, sandy loam scattered with chunks of basalt. Grapevines love these soils and quickly develop deep root systems to sustain themselves in times of drought.

These alluvial flood deposits are not simple soils. They're an intermingling of pulverized granite from the mountains of British Columbia and Montana, Columbia Plateau basalt, and other sedimentary and metamorphic rocks picked up en route. Nor are they uniform: their texture ranges from the finest silt clays to coarse sand and gravel. In parts of the region, the floods laid down extensive beds of gravel, even boulders. When the glaciers that had buried the western lowlands receded, they left behind swaths of scoured rocks and glacial debris, which also varied in consistency—some of them soaking up water like sponges, others exceedingly well drained. Western Washington's vineyards are, of course, planted on the quickest-draining soils.

■ Mountains and Climate

But more than soil affects the quality of Washington wines. In few other wine regions of the world do high mountains have a greater effect on the climate than in Washington. The Cascades, which in the north rise to average heights of more than 8,000 feet, block cool marine air—and most rain—from the interior, helping to create a climate of cold (though not arctic) winters and hot, dry summers. Grapevines thrive in this climate as long as the winters aren't so cold that roots freeze. With a touch of irrigation water now and then, the vines produce superb fruit.

West of the mountains, the deep marine inlets cut by the glaciers cool the shores and islands of the Salish Sea, making it cooler than the Willamette Valley. But marine air also affects some interior regions. By pushing inland up the Columbia River Gorge, which cuts through the Cascades at almost sea level, it cools the Walla Walla Valley in summer and mitigates its winter temperatures, allowing for a longer growing season than either the nearby Pasco Basin or the Yakima Valley has.

■ APPELLATIONS

Is wine made in the vineyard or in the winery? French winemakers, who venerate the *terroir* (a combination of soil, microclimate, and growing conditions), would argue the former. Washington winemakers—not all of whom grow their own grapes—have generally claimed the latter, though their attitude is changing as they get better acquainted with the land and learn which grapes do best where. Not that they haven't always recognized that growing areas play an important role in the quality of their grapes, of course.

When a region has unique soil, climate, and growing conditions, wineries within it may petition the Alcohol and Tobacco Tax and Trade Bureau to designate it an American Viticultural Area (AVA), more commonly called an appellation. (Until recently, this task was performed by the Bureau of Alcohol, Tobacco, and Firearms.) Different appellations are renowned for different wines. It's common to find an appellation mentioned on a wine's label—something Washington winemakers may do, according to law, only if 85 percent of the grapes used to make the wine in the bottle were grown in that appellation.

Because grapes grown in various area vineyards differ widely in quality, the best vineyards are frequently mentioned on wine labels as well. More AVAs should be approved in the coming years, but as of this writing Washington has five. Four of them—the Yakima Valley (designated 1983), the Walla Walla Valley (1984), the Columbia Valley (1984), and Red Mountain (2001)—lie in the warm growing regions east of the Cascades. The fifth—Puget Sound (1995)—lies in the cool western lowlands north of Olympia, west of the Cascades and east and north of the Olympics. Likely to be approved before long are AVAs in Horse Heaven Hills and Wahluke Slope, both in the Columbia Valley, and the Columbia River Gorge.

At some wineries you may find yourself tasting wine right out of the barrel. (Brent Bergherm)

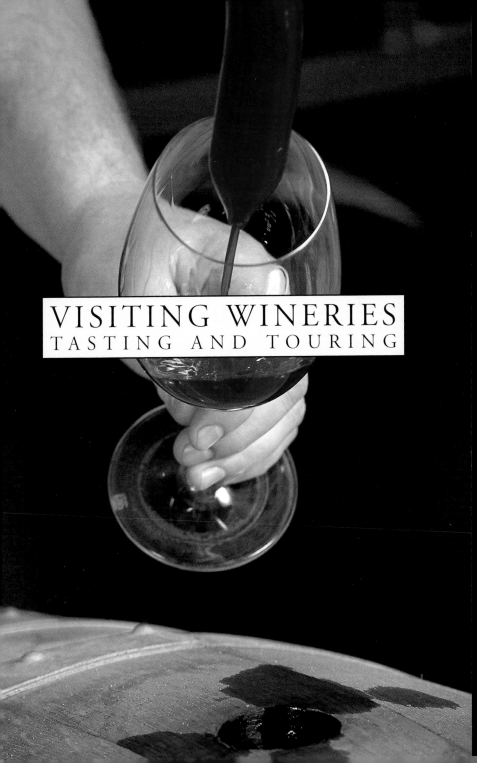

VISITING WINERIES
TASTING AND TOURING

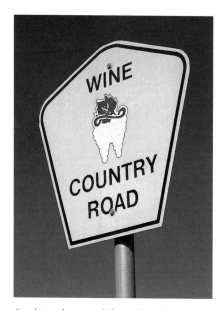

Road signs keep enophiles on the right track.

SUMMER IN WESTERN WASHINGTON. The day is warm and promises to be beautiful. Fair-weather clouds drift lazily across a pale blue sky, a house finch trills its morning song, and the scent of honeysuckle wafts from the garden. As you ponder how best to spend the day, your eye falls on a bottle of wine that you tried yesterday and liked. Learning from the label that the winery is nearby, you decide to pay a visit to taste some of its other offerings and see how the latest vintage is coming along.

As you pull up in the parking lot, you can't help being surprised by the setting: blossoming rhododendrons line the driveway, and a forest of tall conifers surrounds the property and climbs the hillside beyond its outbuildings. There are no vines in sight, except for a few skinny stems and scraggly tendrils trying to climb up the front of a rough stucco facade. Despite a large sign assuring you that this is the place, it doesn't look like a winery. You've visited wineries before and you know what they're supposed to look like. You search for a crush pad or a wine press, vats, and barrels—but you don't see any. Puzzled, you enter the tasting room.

You ask the counterperson where the vineyards are.

Three hundred miles to the east, on the other side of the Cascade Mountains, she tells you.

Welcome to the strange world of Washington wine.

Washington's wineries certainly are different. Quite a few of them aren't anywhere near their vineyards and may not even be in the same part of the state. Most of the areas with wineries do have some vineyards but may not use them for winemaking; the vines have been planted for decorative or educational purposes. The real miracle is that so much of the wine produced by these wineries is so good, often excellent.

On the other hand, when you stop at one of the small wineries in the Yakima Valley or the Columbia Gorge (say, Terra Blanca, Cascade Cliffs, or Marshal's), you're back on familiar ground. These places aren't fancy, but they do look the way wineries are supposed to, complete with vineyards and all the customary wine-making equipment. And you'll know that the winery crushes grapes (instead of buying already crushed juice) if you notice that pomace—the after-crushing residue of stems and grape skins—has been returned to the vineyard as an organic fertilizer.

Most Washington wineries open to the public have tasting rooms of one sort or another. At small wineries they can be very plain—sometimes just a corner of the barrel room, with glasses and bottles sitting atop an upright cask. A plank or two might be laid across barrels. Or a small table or counter may support the accoutrements of tasting, where the winemaker or an assistant pours the wines.

Other small wineries may have a room set aside for tasting (albeit a small one, doubling as a storage room or office), perhaps a small deck or picnic area with benches and tables. A large winery will often have an elaborate tasting room (and a

Wine tastings happen inside or outside, in lounges or at bars, but they are always social affairs.

large, well-appointed picnic area), combined with a gift shop or a deli selling foods that go well with wine. The Bookwalter Winery in Richland has taken the tasting-room concept to the next level by creating a "tasting lounge," where visitors can relax while tasting—implicitly acknowledging that the sip-and-spit method that winemakers and wine judges favor doesn't always work for most buyers, who need a mouthful or two to arrive at an opinion.

■ In the Tasting Room

The tasting room is usually well marked; it's generally a winery's most visitor-friendly feature. Don't worry if you know nothing about wine. Tasting rooms are very relaxed places, designed to introduce novices to the pleasures of wine and give enophiles a chance to expand their knowledge. If you're a novice, everyone will be glad to help (though some wineries hire inexperienced workers, at minimum or near-minimum wage, who know little about even the wines they're pouring). There's no magic to tasting; all you need is a palate and common sense. You evaluate wine by appearance, aroma, and flavor.

■ Appearance

No matter whether it's a white, a red, or a rosé, a wine should be clear, without cloudiness or sediment. Hold the glass up to a window so that natural light can flow through the liquid and show up any cloudiness. Next, the color: is it right for the wine? A white should be golden—straw, medium, or deep, depending on the type. The deepest gold is appropriate in a rich, sweet dessert wine but out of place in a chardonnay or a sauvignon blanc. A rosé should be a clear pink—not too red, and without touches of orange or brown. Usually a brown tinge in a white or a rosé indicates that it's over the hill or that it's been stored badly. Reds may have a violet tinge when young, an amber one when well aged. At that stage it's permissible, too, for reds to have sediment, but the wine should be decanted into a serving vessel—the glass isn't the proper place to let these deposits settle. A definite brown color is a flaw in reds. So is paleness, unless you're looking at a pinot noir; the wine made from this grape can be extremely pale.

■ Aroma

After you've looked the wine over, swirl it gently and stick your nose into the glass. Though a wine's appearance—its color and clarity—may give you a good initial

Rob Griffin of Barnard Griffin Winery samples his product.

clue as to its potential, its aroma may be its most important attribute. Some wines have simple aromas; others have multiple, nuanced aromas. To release the aroma, gently swirl the wine in your glass in order to let it mix with a little air; this will tell you a lot about the wine before you take your first sip.

A wine doesn't have to be complex to be enjoyable. But its aroma should be clean and pleasing. It should never be off; it should never smell of sauerkraut, wet cardboard, garlic, wet dog, or skunk—all odors listed on the official Wine Aroma Wheel of the American Society for Enology and Viticulture, along with moldy, horsey, mousy, and sweaty. Nor should your glass smell of broccoli, bell peppers, or other vegetables—all signs that it's badly made. And it should never give a hint of vinegar, a sure sign of spoilage. You'll also want to sniff for such chemical faults as sulfur or too much wood vanillin from oak.

Fortunately, most aromas in a wine are more appealing. Grapes are a complex fruit, and their fermented juice can evoke all sorts of scents, often at the same time. Look for apricots, peaches, ripe melon, honey, and wildflowers in white wines; black pepper, cherry, violets, and cedar in reds. Rosés are made from red grapes, so they have aromas similar to those of reds but on a more gentle plane—plus raspberry, geranium, and perhaps a touch of pomegranate. Each varietal, or type of grape, has its own distinct aroma. which, with experience, you'll learn to recognize. Wine with good varietal character is better than wine with an indistinct aroma.

■ FLAVOR

After you finish the looking, swirling, and sniffing, you're ready to take your first sip. You'll note that, in addition to flavor, the wine has texture (often described as mouth feel), ranging from light to thick ("full-bodied"). Swirl the wine around in your mouth. Does it feel pleasant? Does it seem to fill your mouth, or is it thin and weak?

Now, the flavor. The human palate can process only four tastes: sweet, sour, salty, and bitter—and salt is not a natural component of wine. If you've discovered some light bitterness in a young red, taste again; you'll discover that the wine's tannic tartness can fool the palate. True bitterness—acrid, unpleasant bitterness—is a fault, but it's rare in wine. Sweetness is a component of many wines, even some that make claims to being dry. Many Northwest wines, even table wines like chardonnay and cabernet sauvignon, have become sweeter in recent years, probably because of the American consumer's sweet tooth. But it's a very light sweetness, barely at the threshold of perception.

When you taste a wine, you'll notice more than just the four basic flavors, of course. That's because your nose plays a bigger role in tasting than your palate does. A taster swirls wine in the mouth, or "chews" it, not only to test the texture but also for the same reason as swirling it in the glass: to release the aromas. The more aromas a wine has, and the more complex their interaction, the more interesting it is.

Next, it's time to evaluate the acidity. All wine has acid; it's necessary to balance the fruit of

The entrance to L'Ecole No. 41.

the wine and give it stability. But it should be an acidity you taste but don't smell. If a wine smells acidic, it has started turning into vinegar. At the same time, taste the wine for sugar. A dinner wine should have next to no perceptible sweetness; a dessert wine commonly has quite a bit. Swallow. Do you like the flavor? Does it relate to the aroma? If not, something's out of balance. Does it go down nicely, or does your throat feel like it's puckering up?

Most important, you should ask yourself if you like the wine. If you don't, then don't drink any more. Though you may learn to appreciate a wine you don't understand, a wine will never really appeal to you unless you *like* it. A wine can be technically perfect, but the parts are less important than the whole, and the whole may bore you. Remember: you're the one who decides. It's your taste that matters.

■ TASTING-ROOM TIPS

There are several other things to keep in mind in the tasting room. Don't overdo it—especially if you're driving. Those little sips add up. And don't feel like you have to buy a bottle just because the winery has given you a taste or two. No one expects you to. Tasting rooms are there to familiarize potential customers with a winery's products. What the winery hopes is that you'll like the wine enough to buy it at your wine shop or supermarket. The things to stock up on at wineries are hard-to-find vintages and varietals—the wines you can't get at home. Sometimes these can be bought only at the winery.

If you're from outside the region, ask about the winery's direct-shipment program. Most wineries ship wine directly to consumers, but only to those in states that allow reciprocal shipments. In 2003, many states liberalized their laws regarding the shipment of wine from wineries to residents, but it's wise to let winery staff make the arrangements. Wineries have to be conscientious, because they face even higher penalties than you do if they ship to a state where it's against the law to do so. They can sometimes make special arrangements to have your wine shipped to a local distributor when it's more convenient or is required by law.

There's another good reason for buying Northwest wines right from the winery and coddling the bottles all the way home: some Northwest wines do not ship well. Even those that do may suffer from improper storage at the distributor's, or at a grocery store's warehouse. Unfortunately—and I write from sad experience—many of the wines for sale even at Northwest grocery stores and wine shops have gone bad on the shelves. It's maddening to open an expensive bottle of wine only to learn that it has spoiled before you could take your first sip.

GRAPE VARIETIES

■ White Wine

Chardonnay
The French grape, widely planted in eastern Washington, where its wine ranges from light to big and complex.

Chenin Blanc
A French grape that makes complex, fruity wine.

Gewürztraminer
A German-Alsatian grape that makes aromatic wine in the Columbia Gorge and the Yakima Valley.

Marsanne
A Rhône Valley grape that produces a full-bodied wine.

Müller-Thurgau
A German vinifera hybrid, widely planted around Puget Sound, that makes a wine with a muscat-like flavor.

Muscat Blanc
(Muscat de Frontignan, Muscat Canelli). A very aromatic grape, with good acids, that makes a rich dessert wine.

Riesling
(Johannisberg Riesling, White Riesling). A German grape that makes great wine in Washington but has been upstaged by warmer-climate varieties.

Roussanne
A Rhône Valley grape from which fruity, complex wines can be made.

Cabernet grapes make deeply tannic wines in the Walla Walla and Yakima Valleys.

Sauvignon Blanc

Dry wine from this Bordeaux grape, fermented in oak, is sold as fumé blanc.

Sémillon

A Bordeaux variety that makes dry, seafood-friendly wines.

Siegerrebe

A German gewürztraminer hybrid that ripens well in cool climates; recent Puget Sound vintages have had great character.

Viognier

A Rhône Valley grape that in eastern Washington makes fragrant wine with a good acid content.

■ Red Wine

Barbera

An Italian grape from the Piedmont; early Columbia Gorge bottlings have been deeply colored and full-bodied.

Cabernet Franc

A Bordeaux grape that produces well-balanced wine in the Walla Walla and Yakima Valleys and Columbia Gorge.

Cabernet Sauvignon

The famed Bordeaux grape grows well in the Columbia Valley and makes deeply tannic wines in Walla Walla and Yakima.

Grenache

A southern French variety that makes appealing, fruity wines.

Lemberger

(Limburger, Blue Franc). A German-Austrian grape that makes pleasing wine in eastern Washington.

Malbec

A red Bordeaux grape that makes softer and less aromatic wine than cabernet sauvignon.

Merlot

A black grape yielding a softer, more supple wine than cabernet sauvignon, merlot has recently experienced a boom, especially in the Walla Walla Valley.

Nebbiolo

The great red grape of Italy's Piedmont region, nebbiolo produces full-bodied, sturdy wines that are fairly high in alcohol content.

Petite Sirah

A noble grape of California, petite sirah has recently been planted, very successfully, in eastern Washington.

Pinot Noir

An ancient French grape that, though it makes some of the world's best wine, is not widely planted in Washington (as opposed to Oregon).

Sangiovese

The principal red grape of Chianti. Yakima and Walla Walla Valley bottlings resemble top-quality clarets.

Syrah

A Rhône grape that produces complex, big-bodied wines; increasingly planted in the Yakima and Walla Walla Valleys.

Zinfandel

A hot-climate grape that in the Yakima Valley and the Columbia Gorge makes big, powerful wines.

■ THE WINE-MAKING PROCESS

In addition to tasting, you should consider touring a winery or two to see how wine is made. Winery tours are particularly informative between August and October, when most of the grapes ripen and are crushed and fermented. At other times of the year, winery work consists of monitoring the wine, racking it (that is, transferring it from one tank or barrel to another in order to leave deposits behind), and bottling and boxing finished wine.

A winery tour is more than just a fascinating diversion, because it shows you not only *how* wine is made but also *whether* a particular winery makes its own. Many wineries still make their own wine (or at least some of it), but a surprisingly large number of them delegate stages of the process to others. The reason is partly economic—to avoid a costly outlay for equipment that may be used only once a year. Instead of growing (or buying) grapes and crushing them as they come in, a winery may send grapes to a "custom crush" facility and then receive the juice (called must) via tanker truck. It may then put the must into vats, fermenting and further processing it as though it had been pressed on site.

Or a winery might go a step further and leave the job of fermenting the must to the custom facility—normally with detailed instructions on how to go about it, what yeasts to use, how much skin contact the grapes should have, and so on; sometimes the winemaker travels to the custom facility to oversee the procedure. Some wineries avoid the growing, crushing, and fermentation process altogether by having their winemaker taste different batches of finished bulk wine available on the open market, buy them, and blend them to create a "custom" or "signature" cuvée. Legally it's even permissible for a winery to leave the entire process, from picking the grapes to labeling the bottle, to a custom crusher—in which case the winery becomes a "virtual winery," serving as little more than a tasting room for wines the owners sell under their label.

You'll also make tours more interesting by visiting different types of wineries. A large winery produces wine in a different way from a small family winery; still and sparkling wines are made by different processes. Most Washington wineries age their wines in refrigerated warehouses; at this time, only a few have caves (pronounced "kahvz," from the French), long tunnels dug into hillsides, where wine is kept naturally at a cool, even temperature. Sparkling wine isn't made the same way

Kissed by the sun, these young cabernet franc vines will grow to full height in a few months.

chardonnay and pinot noir are, and large wineries and small wineries operate differently. Below I've sketched the general process by which wine is made, but you'll find variations at every winery. The best way to learn about winemaking is to visit different types of wineries and compare their methods.

One final note: always remember to double-check a winery's opening hours, either by phone or on its Web site, before you visit. Winery hours vary wildly—and wineries have an annoying habit of changing their hours. You'll save yourself considerable frustration if you take a moment to check before you make the trip out.

■ AFTER THE HARVEST

At some wineries, the grapes are picked by machines; at others, they're still picked by hand—it depends on the terrain and the type of grape. Grapes that will be made into white wine are sometimes picked at night—the fields are lit by powerful floodlights—especially delicate white varietals such as chardonnay. The grapes contain natural fruit acids, which not only bring out the fruit flavors in the finished wine but also give the wine its backbone. Grape acids decrease during the day, when the sun heats the grapes, and increase during the cool hours of the night; picking white-wine grapes at night yields the best acid. Red-wine grapes are a different matter, because so much of their acids comes from their skins.

Workers haul in the grapes in large containers called gondolas. At the crush pad (where tours generally start at wineries that handle all phases of the wine-making process), they unload the bunches onto a conveyor belt, handling them carefully so that none of their juice is lost. The conveyor belt drops the grape clusters into a stemmer-crusher, a machine with a drum equipped with steel fingers designed to knock the grapes off the stems and crush their skins so that their juice can flow off freely. The grapes and the juice fall through a grate, and stainless-steel pipes carry them to a press or a vat. The stems and leaves are recycled in the vineyards as a natural fertilizer.

■ PRESSING AND FERMENTATION

What happens at the next stage depends on the type of grape and the type of wine it's destined for—white, red, or rosé.

The juice of **white-wine grapes** goes to settling tanks, where the skins and other grape solids separate from the clear free-run juice and settle to the bottom. The free-run juice is pumped directly to a fermenter, either a stainless-steel tank, which may be insulated to keep the fermenting juice cool, or an oak barrel.

H O W   F I N E   W I N E   I S   M A D E

Juice that flows from crushed grapes before pressing is called "free-run."

Stemmer-Crusher: Removes the grapes from their stems and crushes their skins so juice can flow off freely.

Wine Press: An inflatable bag that gently pushes the grape pulp against a perforated drum.

Fermentation: The process by which the natural fruit sugars of grapes are converted, with the aid of yeasts, into alcohol. Takes place in large vats or tanks or small oak barrels.

White wines are not fermented with pulp and skins. The grapes are pressed before fermentation. White wines may be fermented in small barrels. They are often cool-fermented to preserve their fruitiness.

Racking: After fermentation, wine is racked, that is, moved to new, clean barrels, to aid clarification. It may be filtered or fined or allowed to settle naturally.

Aging: Many premium wines are aged in small oak barrels. Keeping wine in oak too long, though, kills delicate grape flavors and may make the wine taste "woody."

Red wines are fermented with pulp and skins. Some grapes are pressed after fermentation.

Bottling: After wine has been clarified it is ready for bottling. Very small wineries still bottle by hand, but most bottling is done by machine in the sterile environment of a special enclosure, to keep impurities out of the bottle.

(Fermentation is the process by which the natural fruit sugars of the grapes are converted, with the aid of yeasts, into alcohol.).

Press juice and free-run juice are fermented separately. A little press juice may be added to the free-run juice, to heighten complexity—but not too much, because press juice tends to be too strongly flavored, and some of the flavors may not be desirable. Press juice is fermented in stainless-steel tanks. Free-run juice may be handled differently. In the case of chardonnay and some sauvignon blanc, it's fermented in small oak barrels, in individual batches, separated and labeled by vineyard and lot. At least, that's how the very best white wines are made—and it's why they're so expensive. The process is labor intensive, and the oak barrels, imported from France, are costly and can be used for only a few years. Although French oak is the wood traditionally used for aging wine, many wineries in the Pacific Northwest are starting to experiment with local oak.

Barrel-aging rooms are kept dark, because both light and the heat that lights generate can damage the fermenting wine. Sauvignon blanc and Riesling are commonly fermented in stainless-steel tanks, which may be equipped with wraparound cooling sleeves to encourage fruit aromas and delicacy. Chardonnay, like some red wines, may be, as noted, fermented in small oak barrels, a process that creates depth and complexity as the wine picks up vanilla and other harmonious flavors from the wood. When the wine is finished, several batches are carefully blended together—a step that gives the winemaker a further chance to perfect the wine.

Red-wine grapes are crushed like white-wine grapes, but the juice isn't separated from the skins and pulp during fermentation, because they give the wine its color. After crushing, both the juice and the solids are pumped into vats and fermented together. The must is left on the skins for varying periods, depending on how much color the winemaker wants to extract.

Reds are more robust than whites because fermentation extracts not only color but also flavors and tannins (special acids that help the wine age) from the skins. The fermentation is carried out at warmer temperatures than it is for whites—about 70 to 90 degrees Fahrenheit (21 to 32 degrees Centigrade), as opposed to 50 to 59 degrees Fahrenheit (10 to 15 degrees Centigrade) for whites. As the grape sugars turn into alcohol, they generate large amounts of carbon dioxide, which is

(opposite) Red-wine grapes are crushed like white-wine grapes, but the juice isn't separated from the skins and pulp during fermentation. (following spread) Winemakers taste wine regularly during the oak-barrel aging process.

lighter than the wine but heavier than the air above it, and so forms a cover that protects the wine from oxidation.

As the red wine ferments, the skins rise to the top and have to be mixed back in periodically so that the wine can extract the maximum amount of color and flavor. The winemaker either punches them down manually or pumps the wine from the bottom of the fermenter back to the top, to break up the "cap" of spent grape skins. Punching down—the method practiced in traditional European wineries— is preferable, because it keeps the carbon dioxide cover intact and minimizes the wine's exposure to oxygen. (The fumes, incidentally, make working with wine at this stage potentially dangerous. In November 2002, a British Columbia winery owner, overcome by fumes, fell into a 600-gallon fermentation tank and drowned; his winemaker died while trying to rescue him.)

At the end of fermentation, the free-run wine is drained off; the skins and pulp go to a press, which extracts the remaining wine. As with whites, the winemaker may choose to add a little of the press wine to the free-run wine for the sake of complexity. Otherwise the press juice goes into bulk wine.

Rosé or blush wines are also made from red-wine grapes, but in their case the must is left on the skins for hours instead of days. When the juice has reached the desired color, it's drained off and filtered; yeast is added, and the wine is fermented like any other. Because rosé stays on the skins for a shorter time, it also attracts fewer tannins, making it lighter than red wine. Thus a true rosé is really a lighter, fruitier red wine—not a pink version of white wine. A few Washington wineries indulge in occasional aberrations by making pink wine from blends of white wine, usually Riesling, and cherry or raspberry juice. Others make wines entirely from those fruits, as well as from rhubarb and from apple or pear cider.

■ RACKING, FINING, AND AGING

When the wine has finished fermenting, either in tanks or in barrels, it is racked—that is, moved into clean tanks or barrels to separate it from the lees (the spent yeast, and any grape solids that have dropped out of the liquid). At this stage, the winemaker may or may not decide to filter the wine or to clarify it in a centrifuge. Chardonnay and some batches of sauvignon blanc may be "left on the lees" (allowed to stay in contact with them) for extended periods to increase complexity.

If the wine has been aged for a significant length of time, it will be racked again, and it may also be fined—that is, clarified with the addition of such fining agents as bentonite (a powdery clay) or albumen (egg white), both of which draw off impurities. Some winemakers filter their wines, especially white wines; others only fine them. Wine may be filtered after fermentation, before bottling, or whenever the winemaker thinks it necessary. After white wine is bottled, it isn't kept in storage for long. Most of it goes to a cooperative warehouse, which ships it on demand. At many wineries, only the most special wines are aged in the wineries' own cellars.

After red wine has been racked, it ages in oak barrels for a year or longer. Unlike the barrels used for aging chardonnay, those used for aging reds aren't always new. They may have already been used for chardonnay, which has extracted most of their flavors. Oak, like grapes, contains natural tannins, and the wine extracts these tannins from the barrels. Oak also has countless tiny pores, through which the water in the wine slowly evaporates, making the wine more concentrated. This evaporation creates more exposed surface, so to prevent the aging wine from oxidizing, the barrels must be regularly topped off with wine from the same vintage—another reason that aged wine is more expensive. Some reds are left unfined for extra depth.

HOW TO READ A WINE LABEL

■ TRUTH IN LABELING

A wine label tells the consumer what kind of wine is in a bottle, where the grapes came from, and whether the winery whose name is on the label produced the wine—though it does not necessarily tell the consumer who made the wine. As mandated by the federal government, label information includes a winery (or brand) name; a class or type designation, usually the name of the grape variety; and the alcohol content, correct to within plus or minus 1.5 percent—meaning a wine labeled 13.5 percent could have an alcohol content as low as 12 or as high as 15 percent. (The alcohol content of a bottle labeled "Table Wine" can range from 7 to 14 percent.)

If a single grape variety is named on the label, at least 75 percent of the wine must come from this variety. If an official American Viticultural Area is listed, 85 percent of the wine must come from that area; and if it's labeled a Washington wine, all the grapes must come from Washington State. If a vintage date—that is, the year the grapes were harvested and made into wine—is given, 95 percent of the wine must come from grapes harvested that year. If the grapes come from two or more harvests, the wine must either be labeled NV (nonvintage) or carry no vintage date at all.

If the label states that the wine is "estate bottled," it must also bear the name of the AVA where the grapes were grown and the name of the bottling winery, which must lie within that AVA; the winery must have grown all the grapes used in the wine on land it owns or controls within that AVA; and it must have crushed the grapes, fermented the must, and finished, aged, and bottled the wine on its own premises. The term "reserve," which you'll encounter on some labels, has no legal standing, and may or may not indicate that the wine is from the winemaker's best batch.

Wine that is labeled "grown, produced, and bottled by" has to meet the same criteria, except that the grapes need not be estate grown. On the other hand, "produced and bottled by" indicates that the winery didn't grow the grapes for the wine. "Cellared, vinted, or prepared" means that the winery bought finished wine but aged or blended it in its cellars. "Bottled by" means that the winery bought finished wine and put it (or had it put) into bottles under its name or label. If none of these indications are on the label, it's possible that no one at the winery laid eyes on the wine until the bottles arrived at the tasting room.

If this sounds confusing, buy wines whose labels read "estate bottled" or "grown, produced, and bottled by." But not even these words guarantee quality, since even the best winery can have a bad year. Nor does any of the foregoing mean that custom-crushed wine is necessarily bad—some of it has won prestigious awards.

Alcohol content: By law, this must be listed.

Winery name

Vintage: All the grapes in the wine were harvested in 2002.

Appellation: At least 85 percent of the grapes were grown in the Walla Walla Valley appellation.

Varietal composition: At least 75 percent of the grapes in this wine are sémillion.

Vineyard name: The grapes were grown at L'Ecole No. 41's Seven Hills Vineyard.

Estate grown and bottled: The grapes came from vineyards the winery owns or operates, and the wine was bottled at the winery, with both winery and vineyard in same appellation.

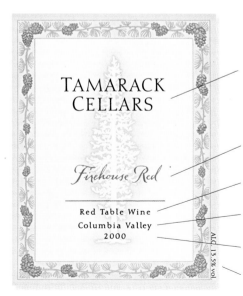

Winery name

Wine name: Firehouse Red is the winery's name for this red-wine blend.

No varietal: No single grape made up 75 percent or more of the wine.

Appellation: At least 85 percent of the grapes were grown in the Columbia Valley appellation.

Vintage: All the grapes in the wine were harvested in 2000.

Alcohol content: Table wines can be between 7 and 14 percent alcohol.

■ TASTE TEST

The only way even the best winemaker can tell that a wine is finished is by tasting it. A winemaker constantly tastes wines as they ferment, as they age in tanks or barrels, and—regularly, though less often—as they age in bottles. Is the wine ready to be moved from fermenters into vats or barrels? Does it need to be fined or racked? Is its color right? Can it stand on its own merits, or should it be blended with other wines from the same vintage? If it's a cabernet or merlot, would it benefit by having another red blended in, to soften it or to make it more complex? If it's a sauvignon blanc, would it benefit from the addition of, say, sémillon? And so forth. The winemaker rarely dares take a vacation until the wines are finished, and the wine is released (winemaker jargon for sent to market) only when the winemaker's palate and nose say it's ready.

Many Puget Sound winemakers are experimenting with pinot noir.

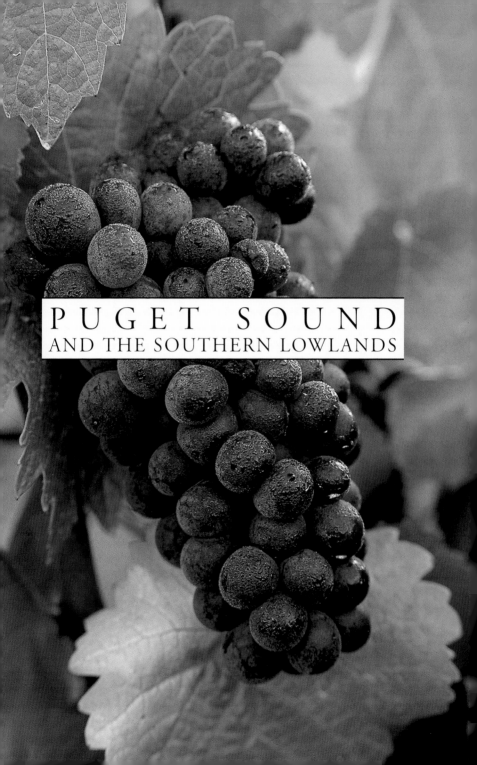

PUGET SOUND
AND THE SOUTHERN LOWLANDS

Cutting oats on Engebretsen farm, near Norman, Washington, around 1907.

SNOW-COVERED PEAKS, GREEN HILLS, BLUE LAKES, saltwater inlets, tree-clad islands, wildflower meadows, grassy pastures, and tulip fields make the areas around the Salish Sea among the most beautiful landscapes in North America. The region stretches from the Strait of Georgia (between Vancouver Island and the mainland) south through Puget Sound, and from Juan de Fuca Strait (between Vancouver Island and the Olympic Peninsula) east through the San Juan Islands to the rugged peaks of the North Cascades on the mainland. In spite of heavy urbanization between Port Townsend to the north and Olympia to the south, much of the beauty of the Puget Sound area has been preserved. The towns and villages of the Salish Sea are civilized places, with comfortable hotels and great restaurants to please even the most finicky traveler.

And this region produces some of Washington's most exquisite wines. Apart from bouts of heat during July and August (and sometimes September), the climate here is benign, which instills complex and multifaceted flavors in grapes. But there's a hitch. The region lacks the steady, intense heat required to grow the grape varieties used to make big, powerful wines so beloved by American vintners and consumers. Because the locally grown grapes lend themselves primarily to delicately flavored wines, many Salish Sea vintners buy their grapes from vineyards in the hot valleys east of the Cascades.

That isn't to say that grapes don't ripen properly on the shores of this inland sea—indeed they do. My garden lies only a few hundred feet from saltwater, in one of the cooler growing zones of the Salish Sea, yet every one of the dozen grape varieties I've planted ripens perfectly during most autumns. Perfection, however, is relative: I don't try to make wine from my grapes, because grapes that are ideal for eating fresh from the vine don't always have the excessively high sugar levels required for fermentation into wine. (If I were serious about finding the right property for a wine-grape vineyard in the Salish Sea country, I would apply the sure-fire "corn rule": if corn ripens well, so will grapes. When you're touring Europe in autumn in search of little-known local wines, you can expect to find them wherever you see ears of corn drying in sun.)

The wines of this somewhat difficult growing region have improved tremendously in the past few years, setting a new, lighter, crisper style. Once America's love affair with big, inky wines has faded, these graceful, highly enjoyable wines will come into their own.

A number of grapes thrive here, as trials at the Washington State University Mount Vernon research station have determined. Müller-Thurgau, a cold-climate white-wine grape widely planted in Germany and, increasingly, in the Puget Sound region and western Oregon, can be almost too productive (over-cropping results in flabby wines); but in the hands of a winemaker who understands this temperamental grape, it makes a pleasant wine with a light muscat-like flavor. In cool regions Müller-Thurgau can produce wine that's similar to Riesling, a perfect accompaniment for fish and shellfish.

Pinot gris, a classic white-wine grape in Alsace, in Italy (where it's known as pinot grigio), and in Germany (Ruländer), isn't yet planted extensively in the Puget Sound region. But it can be quite successful here, making a light yet complex dry wine that goes beautifully with fresh salmon.

Pinot noir, the great Burgundian red-wine grape, is cultivated more successfully in the Puget Sound AVA than many growers think, though much of the excellent wine produced is still in the experimental stage. Plantings in the southern lowlands have also proven successful, and the grape may yield first-rate wine up north once growers and winemakers begin to understand it. This is another great wine to accompany salmon.

Chardonnay, the classic white-wine grape of the Burgundy and Champagne regions, ripens in western Washington around the second week in October, especially when growers have planted clones from cooler growing areas, such as France's Champagne or Chablis (though they may not ripen fully in uncommonly wet or cold years). Some wines made from local plantings have resembled the crisp white wines of Chablis. The climate of the Salish Sea is ideally suited to growing chardonnay for sparkling wines, but these aren't yet widely available.

Gewürztraminer, a classic white-wine grape that originated in Germany and ripens beautifully in Alsace, can, under the Puget Sound's good growing conditions, produce deliciously fruity, full-bodied wines with a spicy bouquet and taste; however, local gewürztraminer is as yet still rare.

A lesser French vinifera grape, madeleine angevine, is frequently planted in the Puget Sound region because it's so reliable, though the wines it produces lack finesse. The best of them go well with local seafood.

Siegerrebe, a vinifera variety created in Germany by crossing madeleine angevine with gewürztraminer, is another white-wine grape that has done well here; the bottlings have been improving with every vintage. At its best, it makes a light, spicy wine that goes well with a variety of dishes, from steamed crab and fish and chips to Mexican food and spicy Asian fare.

Other grape varieties to watch as Puget Sound vineyards expand include auxerrois, a classic French white-wine grape from Alsace; bacchus, a highly aromatic German white-wine grape; chasselas, a popular Swiss white-wine grape; dolcetto, an early-ripening low-acid Italian red-wine grape; gamay noir, the classic red-wine grape of France's Beaujolais region; mélon, the grape that makes crisp white Muscadet and gives a tart, dry wine (a natural match with oysters) when grown in the Puget Sound region; meunier, a red-wine grape from France's Champagne region; pinot blanc, a white Alsatian grape; Portugieser, a red Austrian-German variety that makes decent red quaffing wine; and the noble Riesling, Germany's classic white-wine vinifera grape, which has shown promise in warmer vineyards.

Many of the noble grapes—the varieties such as cabernet sauvignon that produce the best wines—are not widely planted because they need warmth, even heat, to ripen properly, something they may not get every year in cool western Washington. The vineyards here are like those of Europe in that respect, but western Washington's grapegrowers, like most American farmers, want perfect harvests every year. Had French and German growers shared this attitude in past centuries, we wouldn't be drinking their great wines now, because western European vintages are iffy at best; great vintages are few, and often many years apart. Because red-wine grapes need more warmth than, say, berries or apples, the red-wine grape vineyards of the Puget Sound region have been planted on south-facing slopes and in the warmest valleys: on hillsides above Lake Whatcom and in the Nooksack River Valley, in the San Juan Islands, and on Whidbey and Bainbridge Islands.

Grapes have been grown on these islands since the earliest days of the

Point Defiance Park.

Washington wine industry. Wine was part of the pioneer experience—but it was imported wine. Yet as early as 1854, nurseries on Puget Sound listed both American and European grape varieties for sale. Most likely, the majority of these grapes were bought and grown here and elsewhere in the Northwest by home gardeners whose ethnic backgrounds called for wine with dinner.

Western Washington's wine industry got its start in 1872, when Lambert Evans planted American grapes on Stretch Island, due west of Tacoma, in southern Puget Sound. The low, gravelly island became the temporary heart of Washington's wine industry in the latter half of the 19th century. Evans's vines were bearing ample fruit by 1883, and in 1890, Adam Eckert, from Chautauqua, New York, established another grape nursery on Stretch Island. By 1905, the island's vineyards were growing more than a dozen varieties of native American grapes; Campbell Early, later renamed Island Belle, adapted the best to the climate. Some of Stretch Island's vineyards have survived, and some of the Island Belle vines there are now almost a century old.

A 1916 guidebook to Washington State calls attention to western Washington grapes as a special attraction, pointing out that Hartstene Island "maintains one of the largest vineyards in the West, yielding delicious grapes that find their way to distant eastern markets." In 1918 Rudolph Werberger planted a thousand Island Belle and chasselas vines on the Olympic Peninsula at Pickering Passage, west of Hartstene Island. Werberger's winery was one of the few to survive Prohibition, and it eventually became the nucleus of Washington's largest contemporary winery (see Chateau Ste. Michelle, on page 108).

The Stretch Island vineyards were all but forgotten as the vast Columbia Valley grape plantings began to dominate the market. But, though it doesn't produce great wine, Island Belle proved to be a tough grape, thriving despite neglect. There are no longer wineries on the islands of southern Puget Sound, but Stretch Island grapes are still being made into wine by Hoodsport Winery, nearby on the Hood Canal.

By the mid-1990s, western Washington vineyards had established themselves sufficiently for the federal government, through the Bureau of Alcohol, Tobacco, and Firearms, to recognize the Salish Sea region as deserving of an appellation of its own, and one was authorized in 1995. But there are some curious aspects to this Puget Sound AVA: even though the government officially recognizes Puget Sound as "extending about 100 miles south from Admiralty Inlet and Juan de Fuca Strait to Olympia," the area covered by the AVA is much larger, stretching from the Canadian border south through the Cascade foothills to the southern lowlands, and east through the San Juan Islands to the Elwha River on the Olympic Peninsula. Oddly, the appellation includes some marginal areas but omits some wineries (and some potential vineyard sites).

The best way to explore the wineries of the Salish Sea region is in a series of day or overnight trips from Seattle—to the Woodinville wine valley east of the city, to the western islands, to the northern interior; and to southern Puget Sound.

■ SEATTLE

Chatter Creek Winery *map page 101, C-4*

The city of Seattle is home to several wineries that make wine from eastern Washington grapes. Unfortunately, most of the wineries are neither exciting nor consistent in their output. One standout is tiny Chatter Creek Winery. Winemaker Gordy Rawson crafts his wines from grapes grown in southwestern Washington and the Columbia and Yakima Valleys. Rawson has a knack for getting the most from these grapes, and his wines, particularly his cabernet sauvignon, cabernet franc, and syrah, are worth searching out. *620 NE 55th Street; 206-985-2816. Tours and tastings by appointment only.*

■ KIRKLAND

Cavatappi Winery *map page 101, C-4*

Here's the scenario. A restaurant owner-chef breaks new ground in northern Italian cooking. His Seattle-area restaurant becomes so successful that reservations are almost impossible to get. When the chef can't find locally made versions of the northern Italian wines he loves and wants to serve with his food, he starts his own winery—in the basement of his restaurant. To do so, he first has to get state laws changed, which he does. He succeeds so splendidly at winemaking that he eventually sells the restaurant to concentrate on his wines. It may sound like a fairy tale, but that's exactly what Peter Dow did. (The restaurant, Cafe Juanita, operating under new owners, is still good. And the winery is still in the basement.) Dow specializes in such Italian varietals as nebbiolo and sangiovese, which are grown in the Yakima Valley's Red Willow Vineyard. In some years he also makes sauvignon blanc and one of Washington's best cabernet sauvignons. More recently, Dow has also made an excellent inexpensive red table wine. *9702 NE 120th Place; 206-282-5226. Tours by appointment only.*

■ WOODINVILLE

Several important wineries large and small do business 22 miles east from Seattle in Woodinville. From the city, take either Route 520 or I-90 across Lake Washington to Bellevue, where you'll head north on I-405. At Route 522, head west, toward

The late Tom Stockley of the Seattle Times *wrote one of the first books on Northwest wineries.*

Woodinville and Redmond, taking the first exit (after about a mile) and turning south on Route 202 toward Woodinville. Follow Route 202 as it turns west onto NE 175th Street (go right at the second traffic light) and south onto the Woodinville-Redmond Road—the road changes names but not route numbers. At the "Y" where Route 202 turns south, turn north for Di Stefano Winery and south for the other wineries below.

Di Stefano Winery *map page 101, C-4*
The Di Stefano Winery began life in 1984 as Domaine Whittlesey Mark, a producer of *méthode champenoise* sparkling wines. Di Stefano introduced its first wines the fall of 1993, and the success of its complex yet eminently drinkable fumé blancs and cabernet sauvignons soon pushed the sparklers into the background—though small quantities of premium bubbly are still produced. The wines are available at the tasting room, a humble industrial-park affair, and in Seattle restaurants and wine shops. *12280 NE Woodinville Drive; 425-487-1648. Open on weekends. Tours by appointment only.*

Silver Lake Winery *map page 101, C-4*
Silver Lake, which occupies a modernistic cube-shaped building west of two-lane Route 202, the Woodinville-Redmond Road, has been producing hand-crafted varietal wines from eastern Washington grapes since 1989. You can sample both the wines and the company's Spire Mountain Hard Fruit Ciders at the Woodinville tasting room. Highlights include chardonnay, sauvignon blanc, Riesling, cabernet sauvignon, merlot, and a sparkling brut. Silver Lake has also established a satellite winery and tasting room at the former Cover Run winery near Zillah, in the Yakima Valley. The winery is planning a significant expansion to its Woodinville facility in 2004, creating a development on 5 acres to the north of the winery that will be called Wine Land and will include several tasting rooms, two restaurants, and other wine-related businesses. *15029 Woodinville-Redmond Road NE; 800-318-9463. Open daily.*

Facelli Winery *map page 101, C-4*
This small family winery makes great wine in a somewhat incongruous location —in a business park—and the Facellis are people you'll enjoy meeting. Lou Facelli, the quintessential Italian winemaker, knows as much as anyone can about getting the most from eastern Washington grapes; he produces exquisite, highly complex merlot and cabernet sauvignon, as well as superb chardonnay, fumé blanc,

The gregarious Lou Facelli.

Riesling, and the occasional sémillon. Facelli is just around the corner from the valley's two main wineries, Columbia and Chateau Ste. Michelle, and it makes wines as good as either of them. The tiny tasting room is always thronged with visitors, and the sight of Lou signing bottles behind the counter (he's famous for it—he'll even open a case and sign every bottle) is something to behold. *16120 Woodinville-Redmond Road NE; 425-488-1020. Open on weekends.*

Just after it reaches Silver Lake and Facelli, the Woodinville-Redmond Road makes a sharp turn to the left and its name changes to NE 145th Street. You'll see signs for Columbia Winery (it's on the left side of the road) and Chateau Ste. Michelle (on the right).

Columbia Winery *map page 101, C-4*

Columbia justly calls itself Washington State's first premium winery. Founded in 1962 as Associated Vintners by a group of wine-loving University of Washington professors, the winery attracted attention originally with a gewürztraminer but soon branched out into other varietals made from eastern Washington grapes. Over the years, Columbia underwent many changes. It was bought out by Corus Brands, a large-scale producer (which also acquired Covey Run, Paul Thomas, and other wineries), only to be resold in 2001 to New York's Canandaigua Wine Company.

Despite such upheavals, Columbia has maintained its reputation for fine sémillon, pinot gris, chardonnay, and gewürztraminer. Its cabernet sauvignon, from the Otis, Red Willow, and Sagemoor Vineyards, has also attracted attention, as have its cabernet franc, merlot, and syrah—the first syrah made from Washington State grapes. But the winery's best wine is one of its least expensive: the Winemaker's Reserve Johannisberg Riesling. Headquartered in a faux-Victorian château across the street from Chateau Ste. Michelle, Columbia has the state's largest wine-tasting bar. *14030 NE 145th Street; 425-488-2776. Open daily.*

Chateau Ste. Michelle *map page 101, C-4*

This huge winery occupies a beautifully landscaped 87-acre estate first laid out in 1912, as part of a lumberman's weekend retreat, by two of the leading landscape architects of the day, the brothers John Charles Olmsted and Frederick Law Olmsted Jr. Woodinville's first winery, it's still a draw for the region's wine lovers. The winery also calls itself the oldest in Washington State, and in certain respects the claim is valid, though with some qualifications. As a corporate entity, Chateau Ste. Michelle dates only to 1967, but the wine company that introduced the Chateau Ste. Michelle label can be traced back to Rudolph Werberger's Stretch Island winery and several early Yakima Valley wineries. The parent company, bonded in 1934, wasn't known for its fine wines; but the winery made an early jump onto the wine-revolution bandwagon, and today, with its Columbia Crest satellite winery, it is by far the state's largest producer. The wines are consistently enjoyable, and except for a few "reserves" they're reasonably priced. All of them are made from grapes grown in eastern Washington's Columbia Valley, where the winery owns vast stretches of vineyards. Over the years, Chateau Ste. Michelle has

Early morning frost envelopes the demonstration vines at Chateau Ste. Michelle.

established a solid reputation for its Riesling, sémillon, and sauvignon blanc, as well as for chardonnay, cabernet sauvignon, and merlot. The winery also produces reasonably priced Domaine Ste. Michelle sparkling wines. The popular, tree-shaded picnic area can get crowded on warm summer weekends. During the summer, Chateau Ste. Michelle hosts a well-attended performing arts series. *14111 NE 145th Street; 425-488-1133. Guided tours and tastings daily.*

Because the local wineries attract scores of visitors, several restaurants and one luxury hotel have sprung up in the Sammamish River Valley near Columbia Winery and Chateau Ste. Michelle. **Willows Lodge** (14580 NE 145th Street; 877-424-3930) opened with much fanfare in 2001, but though the inn is popular with the software crowd visiting the nearby Microsoft headquarters, travelers used to Napa and Sonoma lodgings have been less impressed. On the other hand, the **Barking Frog** (14582 NE 145th Street; 425-424-2999), the lodge's comfy restaurant, serves excellent food.

The Herbfarm (14590 NE 145th Street; 425-485-5300), a regionally famous Fall City restaurant that burned down in 1997, reopened next to Willows Lodge in 2001. The restaurant still enjoys a cult following, with some reviewers drooling over its nine-course tasting dinners, but it has also come under criticism from others who consider it simply too much. Time (and the state of the local economy) will tell whether the place remains an area institution. Nearby **Molbak's Nursery** (13625 NE 175th Street; 425-483-5000) is not only a great garden center but also a place for lingering over a cup of espresso and a home-baked cookie while listening to the (caged) parrots in the tropical section.

■ REDMOND

DeLille Cellars *map page 101, C-4*

DeLille occupies a pretty "château" across the Sammamish River valley from Chateau Ste. Michelle, its grounds graced by sheep, peacocks, geese, chickens, and trout ponds. A boutique winery, it produces a pricey signature wine called Chaleur Estate Red, a blend of Yakima Valley cabernet sauvignon, cabernet franc, and merlot, as well as a secondary-label red named D2. Also available are Chaleur Estate Blanc, a white-wine blend of sauvignon blanc and sémillon, and a single-vineyard red wine called Harrison Hill. *14208 Woodinville-Redmond Road NE; 425-489-0544. Open by appointment.*

■ SNOHOMISH

The Snohomish Valley, east of Everett and northeast of Woodinville, has no commercial vineyards, but that hasn't prevented one of the state's premium red-wine makers from setting up its base here.

Quilceda Creek Vintners *map page 101, C-3/4*

As Washington wineries produce more and more great reds, keeping your place at the top gets harder and harder. Quilceda Creek has not only kept its place but has also kept its wines reasonably priced compared to others of similar quality. Its truly outstanding cabernet sauvignon has had a staunch following for two decades and is distributed in more than three dozen states and seven foreign countries. The winery produces only 2,500 cases annually, from grapes grown in Columbia Valley vineyards. In the past few years, it has also produced a superb red table wine. Quilceda Creek has remained a family operation, headquartered north of the small town of Snohomish in the home of Alex and Jeannette Golitzin; their son, Paul, and son-in-law, Marv, are also active in the operation. *11306 52nd Street SE; 360-568-2389. Tours and tastings by appointment.*

■ THE ISLANDS

Most of the larger Puget Sound islands have at least one winery, but only those on Bainbridge, Whidbey, and Lopez Islands regularly make wine from their own grapes. In 2002, San Juan Vineyards released the first, delicious batch from its siegerrebe plantings. Read the wine labels carefully if you're concerned about the origin of the grapes made on the islands. The sole winery on Orcas Island, for example, not only produces its wine from eastern Washington grapes but also has them custom-crushed, fermented, and bottled east of the mountains. **Compass Wines** (1405 Commercial Avenue, Anacortes; 360-293-6500), a store en route to the San Juan Islands ferry landing on Fidalgo Island, has an excellent selection of island wines as well as other western Washington bottlings.

■ BAINBRIDGE ISLAND

Bainbridge Island is a short passenger-auto ferry ride from downtown Seattle's Coleman Dock. From the Bainbridge Island ferry dock, take Highway 305 (Olympic Drive SE) to the winery, which will come up on the right after about half a mile. If the weather's nice, you can park your car on the Seattle waterfront, walk onto the ferry, and walk to the winery and back to the ferry.

Bainbridge Island Vineyards and Winery *map page 101, C-4/5*
Established back in 1982, Bainbridge Island Winery did its part to advance local vinifera grape growing by making its wine only from grapes grown in western Washington. Because it's such an easy trip from Seattle to the winery, it attracts many casual visitors. Gerald Bentryn makes light, European-style wines from estate-grown Müller-Thurgau, siegerrebe (a variety he pioneered in western Washington), madeleine angevine, pinot noir, and pinot gris grapes. The winery's fragrance garden is a popular spot for picnics. *682 Highway 305; 206-842-9463. Open Wed.–Sun.*

■ WHIDBEY ISLAND

To reach Whidbey Island from Seattle, take I-5 north for about 16 miles to the Route 525/Mukilteo Ferry Exit and head west about 9 miles to Mukilteo and the ferry landing. Take the ferry to Whidbey Island's Clinton ferry landing. From here, drive north about 2.5 miles on Route 525 to South Langley Road and turn right. Whidbey Island Vineyards and Winery is about 1.75 miles farther along.

The Blackman Bros. firm brought the first locomotive to Snohomish County in 1883.

Whidbey Island Vineyards and Winery *map page 101, C-3*

You can't miss this winery's red barn as you drive from the Clinton ferry landing to the village of Langley. Though the winery specializes in wines made from locally grown madeleine angevine, madeleine sylvaner, and siegerrebe, it also makes a pinot noir from southwest Washington grapes, as well as some wines from grapes grown in eastern Washington. Much like a good gewürztraminer, the siegerrebe wine is pleasantly spicy, making it a perfect partner for Thai and other Southeast Asian dishes. A picnic area near the vineyard is popular in the summer, and so is an old apple orchard on the other side of the winery. Tall Douglas firs complete the bucolic picture. *5237 South Langley Road, Langley; 360-221-2040. Open daily except Tues. June–Sept.; Wed.–Sun. rest of year.*

Greenbank Cellars *map page 101, B/C-3*

This small and rustic winery on southern Whidbey Island occupies a renovated century-old barn. Plantings in the vineyard that borders the winery include Müller-Thurgau, madeleine angevine, siegerrebe, madeleine sylvaner, and pinot noir (which is made into an Alsatian-style wine). Greenbank's white wines are crisp and refreshing. The winery also makes red wines from eastern Washington grapes, and a loganberry wine from local fruit. As at some other Puget Sound wineries, initial bottlings have been pleasant if not quite thrilling, but they're likely to improve as the winemaker gains experience with Puget Sound grapes. *3112 Day Road; 360-678-3964. Open by appointment.*

■ LOPEZ ISLAND

Lopez Island can be reached by taking I-5 north from Seattle to Burlington (about 65 miles). Turn east onto Route 20 and follow it through Anacortes to the San Juan Islands ferry landing—the highway ends at the ferry landing. Take the ferry to Lopez Island. On Lopez, head south on Ferry Road to Fisherman Bay Road to Lopez Island Vineyards.

Lopez Island Vineyards *map page 101, B-1/2*

This family-run winery that operates out of a small stone-and-timber building struggled during its first years, making wine from eastern Washington grapes as well as from its own estate-grown, certified-organic grapes. Recent estate bottlings include a full-bodied madeleine angevine. The winery's siegerrebe seemed a bit

A wooden post marker at Lopez Island Vineyards.

unfinished at first but came into its own with the beautifully crisp fruit flavors of the 2001 vintage. As with just about every other business on Lopez Island, the people here are very friendly. *724-B Fisherman Bay Road; 360-468-3644. Open Fri.–Sat. mid-Mar.–May and early Sept.–late Dec.; Wed.–Sun. June–early Sept.*

For a delectable dinner after your wine tasting, drop in at the **Bay Cafe** (9 Old Post Road, Lopez Village; 360-468-3700), a casually elegant restaurant whose chefs dish up mussels, salmon, and other local seafood, as well as steaks and vegetarian dishes. The menu changes weekly.

■ SAN JUAN ISLAND

To reach San Juan Island, take I-5 north from Seattle to Burlington, a distance of about 65 miles. Turn east onto Route 20, continuing through Anacortes to the San Juan Islands ferry landing—the highway ends at the landing. From the Friday Harbor ferry landing on San Juan, take Spring Street uphill to Second Street, which becomes Guard Street. Turn right (north), then turn right again onto Tucker Street, which becomes Roche Harbor Road, and follow signs to Roche Harbor. The winery will be on your right after about 3.5 miles.

Inspecting grapes at San Juan Vineyards.

San Juan Vineyards *map page 101, A-1*

The tasting room of this tiny winery occupies a century-old one-room school-house. The vineyards and winery were established in 1996, and both are only now coming into their own. Eight acres are planted to madeleine angevine, siegerrebe (a recent bottling shows promise), and pinot noir, with Riesling, chenin blanc, and chardonnay contract-bottled by other Washington wineries under the San Juan Vineyards label. Eight acres may not seem like much next to the huge tracts planted in eastern Washington and California, but the first vintages made from local grapes made it clear that the San Juan Islands are evolving into a wine region to be reckoned with. *2000 Roche Harbor Road, Friday Harbor; 360-378-9463. Open daily.*

Enjoy local wines with a meal at the **Duck Soup Inn** (50 Duck Soup Lane; Friday Harbor; 360-378-4878), an ambitious, inventive, and moderately priced restaurant; or stock up on fresh oysters at nearby **Westcott Bay Sea Farms** (904 Westcott Drive; 360-378-2489) and have a picnic on the beach.

■ THE NORTHWEST INTERIOR

The northwest interior mainland, east of the islands, also contains vineyards and wineries. Pasek Cellars can be reached by taking I-5 north from Seattle for about 55 miles to Conway (Exit 221). Turn left (west) over the overpass toward Conway. After it crosses the freeway, this road turns south. Almost immediately, turn right (west) onto Fir Island Road. The winery comes up on the right after a couple of hundred feet.

Pasek Cellars *map page 101, C-2*

Pasek Cellars began as a humble storefront winery in downtown Mount Vernon but has since moved a few miles south, into a complex of fruit stands and antiques shops near the Skagit River. This is only fitting, since some of Pasek's wines are made from Skagit Valley fruits. Others are from eastern Washington grapes. The blackberry wine is surprisingly good; so is the port. *Tasting room: 18729 Fir Island Road, Mt. Vernon; 360-445-4048. Open daily.*

To reach Mount Baker Vineyards, continue on I-5 north through Bellingham to Route 542, the Mount Baker Highway (Exit 255). Turn right (east) and follow the highway for 14.25 miles, at which point you'll see a big sign.

Mount Baker Vineyards *map page 101, C-1*

Mount Baker Vineyards, established back in 1982, is in the Nooksack River village of Deming. Though it makes some wine from madeleine angevine, Müller-Thurgau, siegerrebe, pinot gris, and a few other locally grown grapes, most of its production comes from grapes grown in eastern Washington. The quality here has improved tremendously in recent years, and Mount Baker now makes house wines for local and fancy Seattle restaurants. On clear days, the picnic area and tasting rooms have splendid views of Mount Baker. *4298 Mount Baker Highway, Deming; 360-592-2300. Open daily.*

Several local restaurants merit attention. Small, cozy **Fino Wine Bar** (804 10th Street, Bellingham; 360-676-9463), the restaurant in the Chrysalis Hotel, on the south Bellingham waterfront, is a fine place where you can watch water birds and the weekly sailboat races while nibbling tapas and sipping wine. The intimate **Oyster Bar** (2578 Chuckanut Drive, Bow; 360-766-6185) serves local seafood as well as steaks; the wine list is extensive, and the views across the water to the San Juan Islands are unparalleled, especially at sunset. The **Chuckanut Manor** (3056 Chuckanut Drive, Bow; 360-766-6191) occupies an early-20th-century home set on the bluff overlooking Samish Bay. Birdfeeders outside the bar's windows are busy, and the food—again, local seafood and grilled steaks—is prepared with care.

■ SOUTH SOUND

South Sound establishments are easily accessible from I-5; Hoodsport Winery is a few miles north of Shelton and reachable via U.S. 101, which connects with I-5 in Olympia.

Hoodsport Winery *map page 101, A-5*

Southern Puget Sound—once the hotbed of western Washington's wine industry—today has only one winery. While grapes still thrive on Stretch Island, near Grapeview, no winery there is currently open to the public. But Hoodsport Winery, on the western shore of the Hood Canal, still makes some red wine with Island Belle grapes from Stretch Island, and offers tours of its Stretch Island vineyard in summer. Hoodsport has undergone quite a transition since it opened, in 1980; known initially for its fruit wines, it now produces mainly vinifera wines. A dessert-style raspberry wine serves as the base for flavorful raspberry-chocolate truffles. *North 23501 Highway 101, Hoodsport; 360-877-9894. Open daily.*

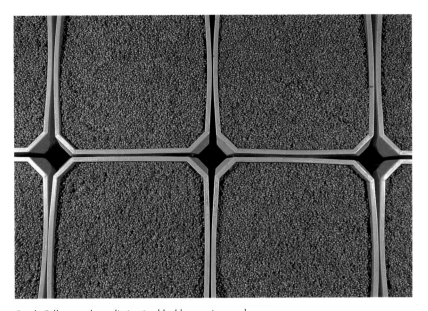

Pasek Cellars produces distinctive blackberry wines and ports.

Pair a Hoodsport white wine with oysters from the **Hamma Hamma Company Store** (35861 North Highway 101, Lilliwaup; 360-877-5811), farther north along the Hood Canal, and you'll have the makings of a delectable picnic.

■ THE SOUTHERN LOWLANDS

At the moment, few grapes are planted south of Puget Sound, but the situation could change as Washington's wine industry expands. The hills north of Vancouver, Washington, at the far end of the southern lowlands, are already one of western Washington's prime grape-growing areas. Geography and climate make this region a northerly extension of Oregon's Willamette Valley, and thus it comes as no surprise that chardonnay and pinot noir do especially well here. Unexpectedly, so does cabernet sauvignon.

To reach Salishan Vineyards from Hoodsport, take U.S. 101 south to I-5 in Olympia and turn continue south toward Portland. (From Seattle, take I-5 south to Olympia.) Continue south through Kelso and Woodland to LaCenter (Exit 16/ North 319th Street), turn left (north) and take NW LaCenter Road into town (about 2 miles). Turn right on Fourth Street and left on Aspen Street, which turns into North Fork Avenue. This road leads to the winery, about another fifth of a mile on the right.

Salishan Vineyards *map page 101, B-6*

The bulk of Southern Lowland grapes are sold to wineries throughout the state, but this winery, established in LaCenter in the mid-1970s, was the first to recognize their special quality. Salishan planted its first vineyards in 1971, making Joan and Lincoln Wolverton true pioneers of the Washington wine renaissance. In the years since their first vintage, in 1976, their wines—especially the pinot noirs—have consistently ranked among the best produced in the state. They're now putting all their efforts into pinot noir—which unfortunately means that they no longer make their superb dry Riesling, which rivaled the best Alsatian Rieslings. *35011 North Fork Avenue, LaCenter; 360-263-2713. Tasting and tours Sat. May–Dec., or by appointment.*

Bottles at Columbia Crest, a pleasant winery to visit.

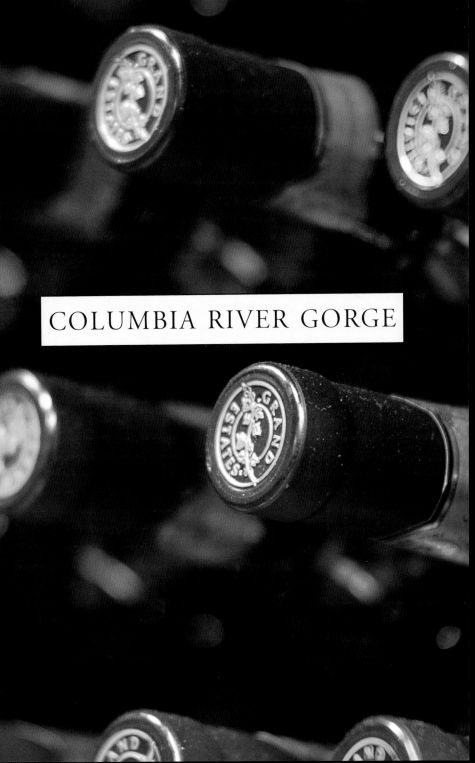

COLUMBIA RIVER GORGE

Lewis and Clark camped at Beacon Rock.

THE COLUMBIA RIVER GORGE WINDS between Oregon and Washington for about 75 miles, with cliffs rising up to 3,000 feet (and in some spots even 4,000 feet) It has two distinct climates—the western end is wet and green, the eastern end dry and golden—and it is certainly one of the most beautiful places in the world. From two spectacular lookout points, visitors can take in the panorama: **Crown Point,** on Oregon's old Columbia River Highway, 11 miles east of Troutdale; and **Beacon Rock,** 6 miles below Bonneville Dam above the Washington bank. You can drive to the top of Crown Point, but to take in the sweeping views from Beacon Rock you have to hike 848 feet to the summit. When Lewis and Clark camped at Beacon Rock, they noted that it marks the head of tidewater, some 160 miles above the mouth of the river. They also commented on the waterfalls cascading down the cliffs on the Oregon side:

> We passed along under high, steep, and rocky sides of the mountains, which now close on each side of the river, forming stupendous precipices, covered with fir and white cedar. Down these heights frequently descend the most beautiful cascades, one of which, a large creek, throws itself over a perpendicular rock 300 feet above the water, while other smaller streams precipitate themselves from a still greater elevation and evaporating in a mist, collect again and form a second cascade before they reach the bottom of the rocks. (*Journal,* April 9th, 1806)

This part of the scenery has changed little since the great exploring expedition passed through the Gorge almost two hundred years ago. But the falls and rapids of the Columbia are gone, drowned by the waters backed up behind Bonneville, The Dalles, John Day, and McNary Dams.

The Gorge was the final, and some say the worst, natural obstacle that the mid-19th-century pioneers who traveled over the Oregon Trail faced. The steep and unstable cliffs made passage by land impossible, and a series of rapids from Celilo Falls (near The Dalles) to the Cascades (near present-day Bonneville) made passage by water extremely dangerous. To reach the Willamette Valley, their final goal, the overlanders had to take their wagons apart and raft their goods and animals down the roiling river. It was a perilous journey, with frequent loss of possessions and livestock and occasional death in the rapids.

The Gorge is still dangerous, because it's still eroding. From time to time there are reports of big rocks falling off the cliffs above I-84 on the Oregon side, damaging cars and sometimes killing travelers. The Washington shore is a bit gentler (though it too has its cliffs, where the road and railroad tracks are obliged to tunnel through), because it's more heavily eroded; landslides have eased its slopes over the past few thousand years.

Beacon Rock stands 170 miles downriver from another landmark, the Wallula Gap, in the Horse Heaven Hills, through which the prehistoric Spokane Floods rushed. (See the "Geology, Climate, Landscape" chapter.) When the torrent reached the Gorge, the water rose to a height of a thousand feet, stripping away all

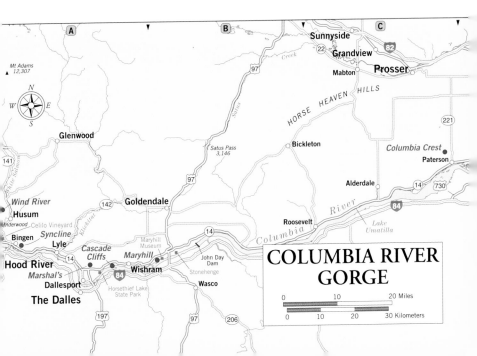

COLUMBIA RIVER GORGE

A view of the Columbia Gorge from Maryhill Winery.

the vegetation and soil in its path. Because of this severe scouring by the floods, the soils here are thin, but they support vegetation nevertheless. The slopes of the western Gorge are clad with forests of Douglas fir, western red cedar (the "fir and white cedar" Lewis and Clark described), alder, big-leaf maple, and Oregon ash. As the climate turns drier, the maples give way to Oregon oaks, the cedars and firs to pines. Still farther east, the landscape turns from forest to steppe, with grass and sagebrush dominating as the trees recede into moist draws. Here the countryside looks much like a giant layer cake scooped out with a giant spoon: the seams and cliffs of dark basalt resemble layers of chocolate; the strips of tan soil and buff-colored grasses look like thick tiers of frosting.

The Columbia Gorge wine country starts near the White Salmon River, which tumbles out of the southern Cascade Mountains and runs east to the southern slopes of the Horse Heaven Hills.

The Gorge's finest vineyard, Celilo Vineyard, was planted in 1983 on a terrace of Underwood Mountain a thousand feet above the Columbia River, at the point where the climate begins to change from cool and wet to warm and dry. (Across the river are the orchards of Oregon's Hood River Valley.) Mount Underwood is a

dormant volcano, and its soils consist mostly of powdered basalt, with the excellent drainage that induces grapevine roots to go deep in search of water. Grapes from the Celilo Vineyard—especially chardonnay, pinot noir, gewürztraminer, and viognier—are used not only by local winemakers; winemakers from Oregon's Willamette and Washington's Walla Walla Valleys search them out eagerly, even though the variable climate of the Gorge ripens the grapes unevenly in some vintages. While the Celilo Vineyard has been called the finest chardonnay vineyard in the Pacific Northwest, its other grapes deserve equal recognition.

Given its geographic configuration, its soils, and its climate, the Columbia River Gorge deserves to be a major wine region, and by the time you read this the Columbia River Gorge AVA will likely have been approved by the federal government. Yet until recently vineyard development here has lagged. During the past decade, more vineyards have been planted, at Marshal's Vineyard, Cascade Cliffs, and Maryhill, as well as farther east at Alder Ridge, Destiny Ridge, and Canoe Ridge.

To reach the first winery on our tour, proceed east on Route 14, and turn north onto Route 141 (alternate) towards Husum. After about 6 miles you'll pass through Husum; a third of a mile farther on, turn left into Spring Creek Road and follow it to its very end. (The route is marked with signs.) If you're coming from the east, pick up Route 141 in Bingen. Reaching the winery is a bit of an adventure, especially if your car has low clearance. The last mile of Spring Creek Road is steep, narrow, and unpaved. As you drive deeper into the woods, you may wonder how anyone could produce great wine in these rain forest–like surroundings—until suddenly you emerge to the sight of an open vineyard basking in the sun.

Wind River Cellars *map page 121, A-2*
The Gorge's westernmost winery hides in the hills northwest of White Salmon. Founded as the Charles Hooper Family Winery in 1985, Wind River is now run by Joel and Kris Goodwillie, and their first vintage (1995) met with the kind of acclaim the previous owners never achieved. The barn-like winery building rises above 12 acres of white Riesling planted in its Silvertooth Vineyard in 1980. Only Wind River's Riesling is made from estate grapes; other grapes come from the Celilo Vineyard, 7 miles to the west. A lemberger made from local grapes is surprisingly big and powerful and has the kind of pleasing acidity that's often lacking in wines from the warmer vineyards of the Yakima Valley and Pasco Basin. Wind River's Port of Celilo is made from Celilo lemberger, and its cabernet sauvignon, cabernet franc, and malbec come from grapes grown in Marshal's Vineyard in the

dry hills above Dallesport, 15 miles to the east. The tasting room is tiny, but there's a spacious deck for picnicking, and sandwiches made by a nearby deli are for sale. On a clear day, you can see 11,235-foot-high Mount Hood looming to the south. The winery makes arrangements with a local outfitter for visitors eager to take in some white-water rafting with their wine tasting. *196 Spring Creek Road, Husum; 509-493-2324. Open daily.*

Retrace your route, taking Route 141 south. Be sure to stay to the left where Route 141 (alternate) branches off from Route 141. This will bring you first to the small town of White Salmon and then to Bingen. Syncline Wine Cellars is in the heart of Bingen, just a block from the post office and Route 14. Look carefully, for it's easy to miss the shed that houses this tiny winery.

Syncline Wine Cellars *map page 121, A-2*

Syncline's production is very small—it made only 96 cases of its 2002 Alder Ridge Vineyard roussanne, and another 96 of its 2001 Celilo Vineyard pinot noir—and its wines usually sell out shortly after they're released. (The wines are released at different times; call for the dates.) If you have the good fortune to get a taste, you'll know immediately why these wines are snapped up so quickly: they're superb. In addition to making a little cabernet sauvignon, merlot, and pinot noir, Syncline specializes in Rhône varieties like grenache, roussanne, syrah, and viognier. *307 West Humboldt Street, Bingen; 509-493-4705. Open on weekends Memorial Day–mid. Nov. Closed rest of year.*

Return to Route 14 and turn left (east). As you drive along the river, you'll notice that the landscape turns drier and the basalt cliffs become more prominent. By the time you cross the mouth of the Klickitat River at Lyle, 10 miles east of Bingen, the trees have receded, and sagebrush and grasses cover the hills between outcroppings of naked rock.

About a quarter of a mile east of the junction of Route 14 and U.S. 197, look for a sign directing you to Marshal's Winery. (If you reach Horsethief Lake State Park, you've gone too far.) Then make an immediate left turn onto Oak Creek Road. The long gravel road to the winery makes for an interesting mile and a half. With luck, you may see—or at least hear—long-billed curlews on the grassy slopes above the road. Be careful not to miss the winery, which is tucked into a steep-walled canyon to the right (east).

On a clear day at Wind River, views include 11,235-foot Mount Hood.

Marshal's Winery *map page 121, A-2*

Marshal's, whose first grapes were planted in 1985, is mainly a grapegrower that also sells a few wines made from its grapes. The winery, which opened in 2001 and occupies a small house, is but a tiny appendix to the vineyards, which run uphill from a low bluff that overlooks the facility and the family home. It's the kind of appealing mom-and-pop operation you used to find on California's Central Coast before that region became famous and prosperous. But though the setting is rustic, the wines aren't. Marshal's makes excellent cabernet franc, as well as cabernet sauvignon, Riesling, and a "black homberg" from vines that are 135 years old—and may well be the very same vines that so pleased Angelo Pellegrini in the late 1940s. (See the "Stepping into History" chapter.) *150 Oak Creek Road, Dallesport; 509-767-4633. Open daily.*

Return the way you came, and turn left (east) onto Route 14. Horsethief Lake State Park has some beautiful picnic areas, but, as in other state parks, alcoholic beverages are not allowed. Continue east on Route 14 for about 3 miles and look for the sign directing you to the next winery, Cascade Cliffs, which lies just off the highway to the right.

Cascade Cliffs Vineyard and Winery   *map page 121, A-2*

There are two kinds of cliffs at Cascade Cliffs: the 400-foot cliffs that elevate the vineyard and winery above the Columbia River (which here becomes Lake Celilo), and the even taller ones that overlook the winery from the north side of the highway. (The lake at the foot of the cliffs covers Celilo Falls, which was an important Native American fishing site until The Dalles Dam submerged the falls in 1957.) The vineyards have the rocky soils that grapevines love, and the weather is hot enough to ripen heat-loving Mediterranean grapes, but the nearby lake water moderates its extremes. This a winery you have to love. The small building that houses the wine-making operations looks more like a fruit-packing shed than a winery, and it's surrounded by vineyards and terrific scenery. And it produces some truly outstanding wines—which, unfortunately, sell out quickly. Highlights include barbera, merlot, and zinfandel, all estate-grown, and a Columbia Valley cabernet sauvignon and petite sirah. *8866 Highway 14, Wishram; 509-767-1100. Open daily.*

From Cascade Cliffs, turn right (east) onto Route 14, and follow the highway about 8 miles to Maryhill Winery.

Maryhill Winery   *map page 121, A/B-2*

At first glance, Maryhill Winery's buff-colored edifice, with its dark brown roofs, looks like it would be more at home in one of California's ritzier wine regions, but it perfectly matches the tan grasses and dark basalt of the cliffs. The vineyards surrounding the winery receive less than 7 inches of rain annually, making irrigation necessary. Maryhill lies in a very hot part of the Gorge, and the dammed waters of the Columbia River provide protection from the regular early and late frosts—rendering the slope perfect for hot-climate grapes like barbera, grenache, malbec, petit verdot, and viognier, all of which have been planted here but are too young yet to give first-rate wine. For now, the winery's focus is on premium reds—syrah, merlot, cabernet sauvignon, sangiovese, and a big estate-grown zinfandel that has a whopping 15.5 percent alcohol content. Maryhill also makes several whites, most notably chardonnay, gewürztraminer, Riesling, sauvignon blanc, and pinot gris, and a blush (cabernet franc rosé). The tasting room (with a deli and gift shop attached) and the picnic area (shaded by an arbor) overlook the river from the top of tall bluffs. It's all very elegant and very relaxing. A large

The setting of Marshal's Winery is rustic, but the wines are anything but.

amphitheater built into the slope below the winery provides the setting for concerts that attract visitors from as far away as Portland. *9774 Highway 14, Goldendale; 509-773-1976. Open daily.*

Returning to Route 14 and turning right (east) takes you first to the **Maryhill Museum** (35 Maryhill Museum Drive, Goldendale; 509-773-3733), whose eclectic collection includes Indian baskets, Rodin sculptures, and Russian icons. After the U.S. 97 junction, you come to a Stonehenge replica. Fill your gas tank before heading any farther east; the cautionary road sign NO GAS FOR 84 MILES is telling the truth. But there are vines. Where the contours of the hills soften, you'll notice the vast vineyards of Alder Ridge, Canoe Ridge, and Destiny Ridge high up on the slopes. These vineyards produce some of Washington State's best red wines.

Some 70 miles farther east, high on a slope above the Columbia River and the intersection of Route 14 and Route 221, sprawls a giant winery, the last we'll visit on this leg of our trip.

Columbia Crest Winery   *map page 121, C-1*

There's more to Columbia Crest, owned by Stimson Lane, Washington's largest wine corporation, than the French château–style winery you see when you enter the grounds: a sizable portion of its facilities lie hidden in vast semisubterranean buildings. Many of the wines made here are sold under the corporation's different labels (Chateau Ste. Michelle, Farron Ridge, Snoqualmie, et al.). The ones marketed under the Columbia Crest label—including chardonnay, Riesling, cabernet sauvignon, merlot, and syrah—tend to be easily drinkable and reasonably priced. The winery is a pleasant place to visit, with nicely landscaped grounds, a small pond, and a courtyard with picnic tables. *Highway 221, Columbia Crest Drive, Paterson; 509-875-2061. Open daily.*

From here, you can turn north on Route 221 and drive on to Prosser and the Yakima Valley, Red Mountain, and Columbia Valley wineries. Or you can continue east on Route 14 to I-82. Turning north on I-82 will take you to the Tri-Cities and the Columbia Valley wine country; turning south will lead you across the Columbia River to U.S. 730, on which you can continue east to U.S. 12 and Walla Walla or west to I-84 and, eventually, Portland.

Merlot grapes are identified typically by their dark blue colors.

YAKIMA VALLEY

Covey Run's Quail label is named after the quail hens that frequent the vineyards.

THE YAKIMA VALLEY IS A BIT COOLER than the Columbia Valley to its north, east, and south, but the region nevertheless produces excellent reds, among them cabernet sauvignon, cabernet franc, merlot, nebbiolo, sangiovese, and syrah. Whites also do well here: chardonnay, muscat, sauvignon blanc, sémillon, viognier, and, in cooler vineyards, gewürztraminer, chenin blanc, and Riesling. Farmers first plowed the Yakima Valley more than 150 years ago, but there's still sagebrush on the driest and rockiest slopes. Now, though, long rows of grapevines snake along the high edge between the irrigated fields on the valley floor and the steppe grasslands of the hills, where the screams of eagles and the cries of curlews resound.

The approaches to the Yakima Valley are dramatic. If you drive in from the west, you arrive through the Cascade Mountains and Chinook Pass (which crosses a flank of Mount Rainier) and the Naches River Valley. Coming south from Ellensburg, you drive through the Yakima River Canyon, a spectacular gorge cut deeply into steep basalt cliffs. Here, white water roiling in deep chasms alternates with pastoral stretches where the river gently purls beneath grassy bluffs decked with wildflowers in spring; hawks and eagles soar overhead, meadowlarks sing in

the meadows, and you may hear the splash of a beaver in a riverside thicket. But approaching from the east on I-82 is almost as scenic. The freeway winds over basalt ridges with views of the snow-capped Cascades, Mount Rainier towering to the west and Mount Adams to the south. Spring wildflowers are thick in these parts, and you might spy a coyote skulking in the roadside underbrush.

The scenery changes dramatically as you descend into the fertile Selah Valley. Tall cliffs hem in the river and highway at Selah Gap north of Yakima, at Union Gap southeast of Yakima, and again at Kiona Gap at the far eastern end of the valley. The massive layers of basalt are exposed to plain view, and most likely they look much as they did millions of years ago, after they surged out of the earth as red-hot magma and hardened into rock.

Yakima is an agricultural metropolis with a renovated old-town area and tree-shaded residential neighborhoods that spread south from downtown. An enchanting riverside arboretum connects to trails winding through riparian woodlands, a

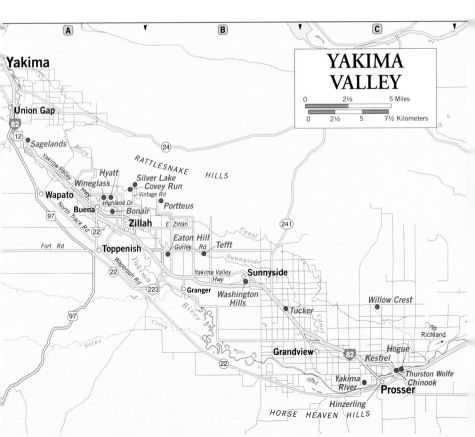

haven for birds—and for bird-watchers, who encounter a great variety of species here, from tiny warblers to huge white pelicans. The exhibits at the first-rate **Yakima Valley Museum** (2105 Tieton Drive; 509-248-0747) include a comprehensive collection of horse-drawn vehicles; a replica of Yakima native and Supreme Court Justice William O. Douglas's office in Washington, D.C.; and a fully functioning, old-fashioned soda fountain that's accessible from the outside and popular with students from the high school next door.

The city has more than its share of resort motels, because Puget Sounders, chilled by their region's often cool summers, flock here to lie in the sun. (Which is why Yakima bills itself as the Palm Springs of Washington.) The large selection of hotels and B&BS make this city a good base for exploring the Yakima Valley wine country. But you won't find any Yakima Valley wineries in Yakima. Officially, the city is included not in the Yakima Valley AVA, which begins east of Union Gap, but rather in the Ahtanum Valley, part of the Columbia Valley AVA. Each fall, Yakima hosts the Central Washington Fair, at whose wine competition judges rate the quality of regional wines.

(above) The city of Yakima, now Union Gap, photographed around 1882.
(following spread) Pioneer Day at Ahtanum Mission, July 1923.

The city of Yakima was founded at the site of present-day **Union Gap,** to the southeast. The budding town moved northwest when the railroad, for speculative reasons, established its own town farther upriver. Seeing their business dwindling, shopkeepers placed their buildings on rollers and, using horses and oxen, dragged them to the new location. Today in Union Gap an old gristmill survives from pioneer days, 19th-century homes rise gracefully from well-maintained gardens, and the fine **Central Washington Agricultural Museum** (4508 Main Street; 509-457-8735) occupies the slopes southeast of town.

Union Gap, with several malls, has recently emerged as a shopping nexus. The city takes its name from the gap in Ahtanum Ridge through which the Yakima River flows into the lower valley. (East of Union Gap, the Ahtanum Ridge becomes Rattlesnake Ridge.) The Nature Conservancy has purchased most of the natural river-bottom woods north of town, with the intention of keeping them undeveloped. These woods, which contain some of the easternmost stands of Oregon oak, also meander up Ahtanum Creek.

The **Ahtanum Valley** surrounding Yakima doesn't have extensive vineyards today, but it's where eastern Washington's wine history started, when in 1847 Catholic padres established St. Joseph's Mission in the upper valley. A church built in 1869 from squared logs still survives. During the following decades, several enterprising vintners planted vineyards nearby. Between 1869 and 1871 Joseph Schanno grew grapes near Union Gap, and in 1871 Anthony Herke, a German immigrant, planted vines near Tampico, east of the Ahtanum Mission. As Ron Irvine notes in his fine 1996 history of the Washington wine industry, *The Wine Project,* some of these vines have survived:

> Soon we discovered grapevines. Some were entwined in the sagebrush, and we could hardly tell their trunks from one another . . . . Some of the vines bore sparse bunches of grapes. I was astonished. This was some kind of miracle. These vines were over a hundred years old, they had never been irrigated, yet they continued to produce grapes.

Scientists from the Prosser experiment station (officially the Washington State University Irrigated Agriculture Research and Extension Station) have examined these grapes and identified them as lemberger, Riesling, muscat, and chasselas.

Later in the 19th century, Gardiner Hubbard, the founder of the National Geographic Society, and his son-in-law, Alexander Graham Bell, planted hundreds of Johannisberg Riesling and mission grape cuttings from California on 6,400 acres in the eastern Ahtanum Valley, near Moxee; but the depression of 1893 wrecked the enterprise before the vineyards could prove their quality.

Yet by 1916, wine grapes were flourishing throughout the Yakima Valley, as a state-published promotional guidebook, *The Beauties of the State of Washington,* enthusiastically pointed out. A photograph in the guidebook shows bushy vines growing taller than the teenage girl standing in front of them. The valley itself is described in purplish prose:

> From the hills on either side, the picture assumes its most perfect
> form. Cities, meadows, orchards, vineyards, hop fields, vegetable gar-
> dens, alfalfa farms, corn fields, and prairies, bisected and crisscrossed
> by railroads, highways, canals, and rivers, protected by the brown
> hills nearby and watched over by the mountains in the distance, sup-
> ply composition for pictures that in detail and variety must discour-
> age all competition.

The present-day Yakima Valley is at an agricultural crossroads. Apples, once the major crop, are on their way out, and grapes are most definitely in. Among the mistakes of the pioneering grapegrowers of the 1960s and 1970s was overplanting Riesling and chenin blanc, which proved hard to market. They rectified the error by grafting over their vines to more desirable varieties or by replanting, and today Yakima Valley chardonnay, cabernet sauvignon, merlot, sangiovese, and syrah are ranked among the world's best.

Support for local wineries took a long time to build when the apple growers reigned supreme, but after a quarter-century of serious winemaking, the valley is finally beginning to recognize the significance of its new industry. The winery boom of the 1980s slowed down during the following decade, though, coming to a virtual standstill after the new millennium dawned and the action shifted east to the hot new Walla Walla wine region. But the Yakima Valley hasn't lost any wineries—so far—and by mid-decade it may even gain a few.

(top) In the apple orchard at D. D. McLennan's Ranch, 1912.
(bottom) A Washington apple orchard today.

■ WAPATO

Yakima Valley wine touring starts east of Union Gap, off I-82, Exit 40 (Gangl Road/Wapato/Yakima Valley Highway, with a sign directing you to Sagelands as well), about 7 miles southeast of Yakima.

Sagelands Vineyard *map page 131, A-1*
The westernmost of the Yakima Valley's wineries occupies a beautiful spot on a gentle south-facing slope of Ahtanum Ridge. Sagelands had its ups and downs until it was acquired by California's Chalone Group (which also owns Walla Walla's Canoe Ridge Vineyards), but its cabernet sauvignons and merlots have now found the masterly touch they needed to bring them to perfection. Surrounded by vineyards and gardens, where roses flourish well into autumn, the winery has an umbrella-shaded picnic area with marvelous views across the valley and the nearby hills; visitors watch turkey vultures, hawks, and eagles soar against a backdrop of snow-capped Mount Adams while sipping one of the reds. The tasting room and shop are in a cedar-and-glass building, originally erected in 1985 as Staton Hills Winery. In a valley where most of the wineries are built in an all-purpose rustic style that makes them hard to distinguish from barns and sheds, Sagelands is an architectural high point—a feast for the eyes as well as the palate. *71 Gangl Road; 509-877-2112. Open daily.*

From Sagelands you can continue east on I-82 into the heart of the Yakima Valley wine country. But the old highway, now known from Wapato to Zillah as the Yakima Valley Highway and, farther east, as Wine Country Road, is far more scenic. To reach the Yakima Valley Highway from Sagelands, continue south under the freeway. The road soon turns east and doubles back under the freeway to follow the Sunnyside Canal for the first few miles. It runs past grassy hillsides where native bunchgrass and sagebrush compete with more recently introduced grasses; in spring or summer, roll down your car windows and you may hear the cry of the curlew, or see hawks circling on updrafts of hot air. As the road winds past hop fields, orchards, and vineyards, you can't fail to get a sense of the valley's incredible agricultural bounty.

The Yakima is an anomaly among rivers, because it flows above its valley, making irrigation easy in the flat land south of the riverbed. But because water refuses to run uphill, irrigating the slopes north of the river is much harder. Early farmers

Sagelands Vineyard merlots and cabernets have earned a steady following.

solved the problem by diverting water upstream, near Wapato, and guiding it south through a canal meandering high above the riverbed.

The ingeniously designed **Sunnyside Canal** maintains a steady but gentle flow of water as it follows the natural contours of the land. The canal, which you can catch a glimpse of now and then as you drive, is the achievement that made agriculture possible on the upper slopes of this semiarid valley. Built mostly with horsepower and human brawn, it was considered an engineering marvel when it was completed, in 1892. The **Roza Canal,** which flows even higher up the slope, allowed the development of yet more Yakima Valley land in the years following World War II.

Unfortunately, this system becomes severely strained in a drought year, when those with senior water rights, such as the farmers whose water comes from the Sunnyside Canal, get preference over those with junior water rights (the farmers whose water comes from the Roza Canal). Fortunately, grapevines have deep roots and need little water to thrive. During recent droughts, the Roza District's grapevines weren't damaged by the temporary shortages of irrigation water. On the contrary, the mini-drought of 2001 appears to have helped to produce a superior vintage—at least for reds.

As you drive slowly through this landscape cut by canals, wasteways, and arroyos, listen for the song of western meadowlarks and the call of valley quail, and watch for ducks, geese, and shorebirds near the water. (A wasteway, in local parlance, is a waterway—creek, slough, channel—that carries irrigation water from fields and orchards back to the river, catching some of the water that might be wasted if it weren't reclaimed and channeled.)

The Sunnyside Canal made agriculture possible in Yakima Valley. This photograph from the late 1800s was taken on the day of the canal's official opening.

■ ZILLAH

The gentle alluvial slopes east of Zillah, whose deep, well-drained soils were laid down by the huge Spokane Floods, are home to several of the valley's most important vineyards and wineries. The roads in this region can be confusing, because they're laid out on a grid but swerve to follow canals, or dead-end at canals and wasteways. Fortunately, the routes to all these wineries are marked with easy-to-see directional signs. Keep in mind that while the postal address of these wineries is Zillah, they're actually up the slope in the countryside, and in some cases quite a few miles west, north, or east of town.

From U.S. 12, follow the signs to Highland Drive (via Buena Road) and, after crossing the Sunnyside Canal, turn right onto Bonair Road. (You can reach Bonair and Wineglass Cellars a little more quickly from I-82 by taking Exit 50—Route 22, the Buena exit—and following the signs to the wineries.)

Bonair Winery *map page 131, A-2*
Bonair Winery, the only half-timbered building in this neck of the orchards, lies just north of a bend in the Sunnyside Canal. The winery was founded in 1985, when Yakima native and amateur winemaker Gail Puryear graduated from home winemaking to a more challenging professional career. Bonair has held its own in a competitive market, with buttery chardonnays and big reds. Its Riesling, produced in smaller quantities, caters to softer palates. A picnic area with a gazebo and a koi pond invites visitors to linger. *500 South Bonair Road; 509-829-6027.*

From Bonair, drive back across Highland Drive, heading north, and look for Wineglass Cellars on the left.

Wineglass Cellars *map page 131, A-2*
After the half-timbered stylishness of Bonair, the look of Wineglass Cellars comes off as decidedly utilitarian—this could just as easily be a fruit-packing operation or a creamery as a winery—but the wines, produced in small lots, are hardly commonplace. In addition to the almost de rigueur chardonnay, the highlights here include cabernet sauvignon and zinfandel. Other superior wines include a lush reserve merlot; a reasonably priced blend called Capizimo (perfect for a barbecue), made from zinfandel, cabernet sauvignon, and merlot; and a robust blend called Rich Harvest. This last wine, a made from cabernet sauvignon, merlot, and cabernet franc, can hold up to any cut of beef, lamb, or game. *260 North Bonair Road; 509-829-3011. Open on weekends mid-Feb.–Nov.*

Leaving Wineglass Cellars, turn left (north) onto Bonair Road; after about a mile, turn right onto Gilbert Drive. You can't miss Hyatt Vineyards, about 1.5 miles farther along on the right.

Hyatt Vineyards *map page 131, A-2*

Hyatt Vineyards is big in a physical as well as an enological sense, comprising 97 acres of estate vineyards. Established in 1985, the winery, owned by Leland and Linda Hyatt, has always been well respected locally for its merlot and cabernet sauvignon, but lately those wines have been attracting national attention. The late-harvest Riesling here is also worth tasting. The winery has spacious grounds for picnicking. On clear days, spectacular views of the Yakima Valley, Mount Adams, and the Cascade Mountains can be had. *2020 Gilbert Road; 509-829-6333. Open daily Mar.–Jan., weekends only in Feb.*

Continue east and turn right onto Roza Drive. A left onto Highland Drive and another left onto Vintage Road will take you to Silver Lake Winery at Roza Hills. But a short detour into Zillah is worth your while. Roza Drive turns into Fifth Street and dead-ends on First Avenue, Zillah's main drag. (A century-old wood-frame church sits near the junction of Fifth Street and First Avenue.)

Zillah's corner store and drugstore in the early 1900s.

Turn left on First Avenue to reach the **Squeeze Inn** (611 East First Avenue; 509-829-6226), one block to the east, on the left side of the street. An unpretentious, reasonably priced family-operated establishment that's been around since 1932, the Squeeze Inn looks as timeworn as the surrounding structures on Zillah's main street. At its white-tablecloth dining room the big draws are prime rib and steaks, soups and salads, and fresh seafood. The hearty breakfasts and lunches are popular with local grapegrowers and winemakers.

First Avenue also takes you to **El Ranchito** (1319 East First Avenue; 509-829-5880), at the east end of town, just off U.S. 12/I-82. This large cafeteria-style Mexican restaurant, tortilla factory, deli, and import shop is a favorite hangout for locals, visitors, and seasonal farmworkers. The food is good and inexpensive. (You can also get a tasty Mexican lunch at any of the many taco trucks that pop up throughout the valley at midday.) A short distance from El Ranchito, on Wine Country Road east of Zillah, the **Teapot Dome Gas Station** is a nutty landmark. This unique service station—which still pumps gas—was built in the shape of teapot (replete with spout) to commemorate the Teapot Dome oil scandal of the early 1920s.

Teapot Dome Gas Station is one of the country's oldest working gas stations.

Zillah's main-street business district, most of its storefronts dating from the early 20th century, is perched dramatically on bluffs above the Yakima River. A post-prandial stroll here is a pleasure, especially in autumn, when the colors of the foliage blaze up from the valley below town.

If you have extra time, you might take another detour to the small town of **Toppenish,** on the south (Yakama Nation) side of the river. Toppenish is well known for its Western cowboy atmosphere and for the murals decorating the walls of its downtown buildings. Since 1989, when the Toppenish Mural Association began commissioning artworks to attract commerce, artists from the region have completed more than 40 colorful paintings, in a variety of styles, commemorating the town's history and spirit. You can view the murals and wander through crafts and antiques shops, visit the **Hops Museum** (22 South B Street; 509-865-4677), or, south of town, stop by the **Yakama Nation Cultural Center** (U.S. 97; 509-865-2800), which has a fascinating tribal museum, a gift shop, a restaurant, and a long-house where cultural events, including traditional dance performances, are held.

Close to the Cultural Center is the **Yakama Nation Legends Casino** (580 Fort Road; 509-865-8800), owned by the Yakama Indian Nation but more popular with nonnative gamblers.

Return to Highland Drive via Fifth Street/Roza Drive. Turn right on Highland Drive, then left on Vintage Road and follow the signs to Silver Lake Winery at Roza Hills.

Silver Lake Winery at Roza Hills   *map page 131, A-2*

This modern winery, high on a slope overlooking vineyards, orchards, and the Yakima Valley, started up in 1982, when a group of local fruit growers, with high hopes for the wine market, founded it as Quail Run. Their winery never hit its stride, and having to change its name to Covey Run in the late 1980s, to avoid conflict with California's Quail Ridge winery, didn't improve matters. The winery floundered along under its new name for another decade until Corus Brands, the parent company of Woodinville's Columbia Winery, acquired it. When the giant Canandaigua Wine Company bought Corus, Covey Run began being made at a Sunnyside bulk facility. Woodinville's Silver Lake Winery leased the winery build-ing and now makes some wine here. The views from the winery and its picnic area, sweeping across the valley to the Cascades and Mount Adams, are breathtaking. If you climb the slope behind the parking area, you'll come upon a concrete channel filled with swiftly flowing water: the Roza Canal, which carries irrigation water

Murals like this one decorate the exterior walls of many buildings in downtown Toppenish.

from the Yakima River Canyon to the Roza Slope of the lower Yakima Valley. Curlews cry in the hills during spring and early summer; year-round you can spot soaring hawks and, with luck, golden eagles. *1500 Vintage Road; 509-829-6235. Open daily.*

Return to Highland Drive and follow it east for three-quarters of a mile to a sharp turn in the road. Signs will direct you to Portteus Winery.

Portteus Winery *map page 131, A/B-2*

A passion for wine brought Paul Portteus III from Seattle to the Yakima Valley in 1980. Two years later, he and his wife, Marilyn, planted the first 8 acres of a 47-acre vineyard to red-wine grapes. Besides cabernet sauvignon, cabernet franc, and syrah, their vineyard had the only plantings of zinfandel in Washington until several Columbia Gorge growers planted this California grape in the late 1990s. Portteus sells 75 percent of its grapes; some of Washington's best reds have come from its vineyard. The winery's zinfandel and cabernet sauvignon have a local cult following—it produced its first cabernet sauvignon from the 1984 vintage—but while the wines are solid, they sometimes lack depth and complexity (That's not necessarily the case with wines made from Portteus grapes by other wineries, such as Quilceda Creek.) *5201 Highland Drive; 509-829-6970. Open daily.*

■ GRANGER

From Portteus, return to Highland Drive; continue east two-tenths of a mile to Lucy Lane and turn left (south). After about 2 miles, turn left onto East Zillah Road, right onto Thacker Road, and left onto Gurley Road, which will take you to Eaton Hill Winery.

Eaton Hill Winery *map page 131, B-2*
This small winery has been making good wines without much fanfare since University of Washington scientist Edward Stear and his wife, JoAnn, opened it in 1988. The winery building began life in the early 1900s as a fruit and vegetable cannery operated by farmer and master builder Floyd Rinehold, who built his

Concrete dinosaurs populate a park in the small town of Granger.

farmhouse around the same time. The resident winemaker, Gary Rogers, turns out noteworthy cabernet sauvignon, chardonnay, muscat canelli, sémillon, and gewürztraminer, as well as Rainier cherry wine, a malvasia, and a port-style cabernet. *530 Gurley Road; 509-854-2220. Open daily.*

A short detour from Eaton Hill will bring you to **Granger,** a small farming town just off I-82, about halfway between Zillah and Sunnyside. Its tree-shaded streets provide a respite from the summer heat of the valley floor. The town takes its name from Walter Granger, an engineer who, starting in 1892, dug the first 25 miles of the Sunnyside Canal. Granger's population is mostly Hispanic; local workers tend nearby apple and cherry orchards, vineyards, and hop fields. In recent years, large dairies have moved into the area, sending milk to the Darigold cheese plant in nearby Sunnyside. While the region's wineries attract adult visitors, children flock to a unique set of 15 **concrete dinosaurs,** ranging in height from 4 to 15 feet and suitable for crawling all over, in a park playground near the freeway. The **H. L. Worden Co.** (118 Main Street; 509-854-1557) fabricates Tiffany-style stained-glass lamp kits and ships them nationwide, but the selection is best at the factory, where the showroom has lamp displays and also sells art glass for making lamps.

■ OUTLOOK

East of Eaton Hill, Gurley Road turns into Independence Road and crosses the Sunnyside Canal to take you to Tefft Cellars, which is in the town of Outlook.

Tefft Cellars *map page 131, B-2*

This small winery makes drinkable wines at affordable prices. Besides turning out wines from Yakima Valley standards—chardonnay, chenin blanc, gewürztraminer, cabernet sauvignon, cabernet franc, syrah, and zinfandel—Joel Tefft, the owner and winemaker, also pays attention to less common grape varieties, among them marsanne, sangiovese, viognier. He makes an Italian-style pinot grigio from locally grown pinot gris grapes, as well as Bordeaux blends, Chianti-style wines, rosés, late-harvest dessert wines, ice wine, and berry ports. The Teffts recently built themselves a new house and converted their old home into a bed-and-breakfast, called the Outlook Inn. *1320 Independence Road, Outlook; 509-837-7651. Open daily.*

From Tefft, take Outlook Road south to U.S. 12 and follow the highway into Sunnyside (where it becomes Lincoln Avenue).

■ SUNNYSIDE

The largest town in the middle Yakima Valley, this commercial center has the usual chain stores and strip malls along its outskirts, but it also has an exceptionally well-preserved downtown area, with many buildings dating from the late 19th and early 20th centuries. The sagebrush and bunchgrass slopes of Snipes Mountain, which overlooks the town, became a residential neighborhood of tree-shaded homes with wide lawns early in the past century, when a local developer had the bright idea of pumping water to the top of the mountain.

Sunnyside's oldest structure, a log cabin built in 1859 by the self-proclaimed cattle king Ben Snipes, has recently been refurbished. Said to be the oldest cabin built by white settlers in the Yakima Valley, it is indeed a decade older than St. Joseph's Mission in the Ahtanum Valley. The cabin stands across the street from the **Sunnyside Museum** (704 South Fourth Street; 509-837-6010), which houses a collection of late-19th- and early-20th-century household items, along with many historical photographs.

The town has several good restaurants and inns, among them the **Snipes Mountain Brewery** (905 Yakima Valley Highway; 509-837-2739), which serves hearty steaks and burgers and the sausage dishes that have become common at microbreweries. Locals like the Mexican food at **El Conquistador** (612 East Edison Avenue; 509-839-2880). What's now the **Sunnyside Inn Bed & Breakfast** (800 East Edison Avenue; 509-839-5557) was built in 1919 by a doctor and his wife as an examining room and family residence.

Somehow, Sunnyside missed out on the wine revolution of the 1970s, even though the farm of one of the Valley's pioneering grapegrowers, the Tuckers, lies only a few miles east of town. But the Washington vinifera revolution *could* have happened here, and decades before it did. The man who nearly made it happen, William Beamer Bridgman, was a Canadian who moved to the Yakima Valley in 1902. He became an expert in drainage law, wrote many of the irrigation statutes for Washington State, and served two terms as the mayor of Sunnyside. Bridgman planted his first vinifera grapes in 1917, on Snipes Mountain, but his first crop matured just in time for Prohibition, which began in 1920, and so he had to sell his grapes to home winemakers.

With the repeal of Prohibition in 1933, Bridgman started his own winery, but although he worked hard to market his wines nationally, they couldn't compete with California wines either in price or quality. (There's also anecdotal evidence that they

A barn alongside the Sunnyside Canal.

weren't all that good.) However, Bridgman's early efforts inspired Dr. Walter Clore, a horticulturist in Prosser, to begin a lifelong study of grapegrowing. Together, Bridgman and Clore provided the cuttings for many of the vineyards planted in eastern Washington in the 1950s. Bridgman eventually sold his winery and vineyards; he died in 1968, just as the Washington wine industry was gearing up. The vineyards he planted are still producing premium grapes, which suggests that it was the quality not of the area's grapes but rather of the winemaking that held back Washington's wine industry for so long. Today, one of the state's best wineries, Washington Hills Cellars, honors Bridgman with a special label.

Washington Hills Cellars/Apex/Bridgman Cellars *map page 131, B-2/3*
The genius behind Washington Hills is Harry Alhadeff, long one of Seattle's most respected wine merchants. Working with Brian Carter, one of the state's top winemakers, he has produced a string of respectable, reasonably priced wines. Bridgman Cellars' wines are a step above the Washington Hills ones, and those released under the Apex name are, as you might guess from the name, at the high end. But this is not to denigrate the wines of Washington Hills in any way: these

These Yakima Valley signs identify the roads but also the importance of winemaking here.

bottlings, especially the whites, have shown remarkable consistency. The winery, which occupies a former dairy plant, has a tasting room, a gift shop, and a grassy picnic area. *111 East Lincoln Avenue; 509-839-9463. Open daily.*

From Washington Hills, continue east on Lincoln Avenue to U.S. 12. The entrance to Tucker Cellars is on the left (north) side of the highway.

Tucker Cellars *map page 131, B-3*

The Tucker family came to the Yakima Valley as sharecroppers during the Great Depression but soon became successful farmers and were among the first to grow vinifera grapes on a commercial scale. Dean and Rose Tucker founded the winery in 1981; both it and the estate vineyards are family operations involving their four children—Mike, John, Deanna, and Randy, who's the winemaker. Tucker plantings include Riesling, pinot noir, gewürztraminer, chenin blanc, chardonnay, and muscat canelli. Attached to the Tucker Cellars tasting room is the family's produce stand, which sells, in season, some of the Yakima Valley's best fruits and vegetables. There's a picnic area. *70 Ray Road/U.S. 12; 509-837-8701. Open daily.*

■ PROSSER

From Tucker Cellars, continue east on U.S. 12 to I-82 and head east toward Prosser. Take the first Prosser exit—Exit 80, Gap Road—and turn left (north) to reach Willow Crest Winery.

Willow Crest Winery *map page 131, C-3*

Willow Crest, another small family winery, occupies a renovated farmhouse tucked into acres of vineyards on gentle slopes north of Prosser. Wines made here include a pinot gris, a dry gewürztraminer, a merlot–cabernet sauvignon blend called Red One, and some late-harvest wines. The picnic area offers a panoramic view of the lower Yakima Valley. *55002 North Gap Road; 509-786-7999. Open on weekends.*

Return to Prosser via Gap Road (about 5.25 miles). As this road crosses I-82, the name changes to Wine Country Road. Follow it south for about a mile, then turn right onto West North River Road and follow that for about a mile to the Yakima River Winery.

Yakima River Winery *map page 131, C-3*

New York transplant John W. Rauner founded this winery in 1978, and it produced good wines from the start. Initial production leaned heavily on whites, among them fumé blanc, but in recent years the winery has become known for its barrel-aged cabernet sauvignon, merlot, and lemberger. The vintage port has acquired a cult following. *143302 West North River Road; 509-786-2805. Open daily.*

Return to Gap Road; turn right onto Wine Country Road; and, after crossing the river, go left at the fork in the road onto Sherman Street. Follow Sherman Street to the Hinzerling Winery, which stands at the intersection of Sherman Street and Sheridan Avenue.

Hinzerling Winery *map page 131, C-3*

In a region of winemakers who stubbornly hold the opinion that you don't need a glitzy winery to make great wine, it's only right that the valley's oldest family-owned-and-operated winery still occupies the grungy old auto-repair shop it started out in. For almost 30 years winemaker Mike Wallace has produced some of the valley's best wines, in small, boldly flavored lots. His triumphs include a dry gewürztraminer, full-bodied reds that age well, ports, sherries, and other dessert and late harvest-wines. *1520 Sheridan Avenue; 509-786-2163. Open daily.*

(following pages) A hot-air-balloon ride provides an enchanting perspective on the valley's terrain.

In January 2001, Wallace and his family bought an old house that had been marked for demolition, moved it to an empty lot next to the winery, and restored it. That summer they opened it as the **Vintner's Inn** (1524 Sheridan Avenue; 509-786-2163), a restaurant and B&B.

Prosser got its start in 1887 with a flour mill that stood at the east end of town, at the Yakima River Falls, a favorite Native American fishing site. The town soon developed into a fruit and vegetable canning and shipping center, and grew prosperous—as you can tell from a stroll down its tree-shaded streets, which are lined with the beautiful homes of local farmers and merchants.

Prosser is the seat of Benton County, and the **County Court House** (620 Market Street), a brick structure built in 1926, has an impressive central portico with fluted classical columns.

While you're downtown, a pleasant stop for lunch or dinner is the **Blue Goose Restaurant** (306 Seventh Street; 509-786-1774), which serves all-American family fare—prime rib, steaks, seafood, Italian dishes, and decadent desserts. It also has the lower Yakima Valley's most extensive local wine list.

The chalkboard at the Vintner's Inn lists different vintages each day.

Prosser was at the forefront of the Yakima Valley wine revolution of the 1970s, in large part because the Washington State University agricultural experiment station north of town had demonstrated that wine grapes could be grown successfully in local soils. Several more wineries lie east of town, in or near the Port of Benton's Prosser Wine and Food Park. The industrial facades of the buildings belie the quality of the wines produced in them.

After visiting Hinzerling, continue east on Sherman, across I-82. The white farmhouse at the right is the home of Chinook Wines.

Chinook Wines *map page 131, C-3*

Chinook is the highly successful venture of husband-and-wife team Clay Mackey (grape grower) and Kay Simon (winemaker), who began it in 1983 in a small farmhouse shaded by cherry trees. Mackey and Simon have an uncanny knack for coaxing the most out of locally grown grapes. Chinook makes its chardonnay, sauvignon blanc, sémillon, cabernet franc, cabernet sauvignon, and merlot entirely from Yakima Valley grapes. A shady picnic area behind the tasting room is a blissful place to enjoy a chilled glass of wine on a hot day. *Wine Country Road at Wittkopf Loop; 509-786-2725. Open on weekends, May–Oct.*

Beyond Chinook, the cherry orchards give way to packing houses, which are separated by I-82 from the grassy slopes of the Horse Heaven Hills to the south. The wineries, tucked between the huge fruit warehouses, are well marked and easy to find. The westernmost was also one of the first.

Hogue Cellars *map page 131, C-3*

The large slab building housing the Hogue Cellars may look industrial, but the wines are far from it. The Hogues, one of the lower Yakima Valley's most prominent farming families, were better known for their apples, Concord grapes, hops, mint, and other crops when they started their winery in 1982. But their reputation soon extended to their wines. The first was a Johannisberg Riesling, and they've gone on to make stellar sémillon and fumé blanc. In recent years the emphasis has shifted to big reds: cabernet sauvignon, merlot, and a blend made from the two grapes. The Hogues also make pickled asparagus, green beans, and other foods, all for sale in the gift shop attached to the winery's tasting room. Vincor International purchased the Hogue Cellars winery and grounds in 2001, but the Hogues kept their vineyards—so they're still growing the grapes, even though they no longer make the wine. *Wine Country Road; 509-786-4557. Open daily.*

Thurston Wolfe Winery *map page 131, C-3*

Wade Wolfe is one of the Yakima Valley's most respected enologists. He makes his living mainly by working for local wineries, but he and his wife, Becky Yeaman, started a winery of their own in Yakima in 1987. The winery moved east, to Prosser, in 1996, when Wolfe took a job with the Hogue Cellars. It now occupies a small storefront east of the Hogue Cellars in the Port of Benton's Prosser Wine and Food Park. In recent years, Thurston Wolfe ("Thurston" is Wolfe's mother's maiden name) has produced noteworthy red table wines, as well as port and dessert wine made from black muscat grapes. *2880 Lee Road, Suite C; 509-786-1764. Open Thur.–Sun., Apr.–mid-Dec.*

Kestrel Vintners *map page 131, C-3*

In only a few years, Kestrel has established itself as one of the Yakima Valley's premium wineries. Although visiting the winery, in the Port of Benton's Prosser Wine and Food Park, doesn't necessarily rank as a great sensory pleasure, tasting the wines does. Kestrel makes mainly reds (cabernet sauvignon, merlot, syrah), as well as some whites (chardonnay, viognier), from grapes—some of them estate-grown—that are deliberately stressed to increase the intensity of their flavors. The tasting room sells cheeses and deli items to go with the wines. *2890 Lee Road; 509-786-2675. Open on weekends.*

The easternmost Yakima Valley wineries have their own appellation, Red Mountain, covered in the next chapter.

Wine casks line the corridor at Terra Blanca Vintners.

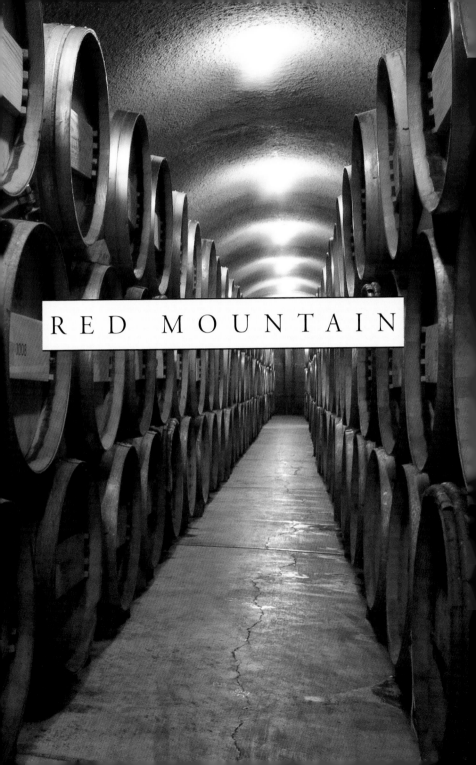

RED MOUNTAIN

Red Mountain is particularly hospitable to cabernet sauvignon, merlot, and syrah grapes.

EAST OF PROSSER, THE YAKIMA VALLEY CONSTRICTS, and more and more basalt breaks out from under the soft silt, rising as cliffs above the Yakima River and on the northern slopes of the Horse Heaven Hills. At narrow Kiona Gap, where the river squeezes through the cliffs, the railroad and the I-82 freeway cling to the side of the slopes, one above the other.

At Kiona, the Yakima River takes a sharp turn northward to Horn Rapids, then turns south again past West Richland, and flows southeast to merge with the Columbia River between the cities of Richland and Kennewick (some 10 miles above the mouth of the Snake, which enters the Columbia on the opposite shore, south of Pasco). Sere Rattlesnake Ridge, which rises to a height of more than 2,000 feet, separates the Yakima and the Columbia Valleys. Locals claim that Rattlesnake Mountain, at 3,450 feet, is the tallest treeless mountain in the western hemisphere—though the slopes are in fact anything but barren: native bluebunch wheatgrass grows to a height of more than 3 feet, and big sagebrush may grow more than 10 feet tall. In spring, the slopes are brightly painted blue, yellow, white, lavender, and pink by flowering lupine, balsamroot, goldenweed, phlox, and fleabane respectively.

Red Mountain rises within that big northern bend of the Yakima River. At 1,253 feet, it's hardly the area's tallest mountain—it's really more of a low, rounded ridge than a peak or a butte—and you may fail to note any distinguishing features. But Red Mountain has vineyards as well as sage and grass, and most of them are situated on its southwestern slopes. Because this is a warm growing area, red-wine vines, cabernet sauvignon, merlot, and syrah among them, predominate. What makes Red Mountain special isn't its topography but its soil and its climate. The soil is some of the most powdery in the state. And the Yakima River assures rapid nightly cooldowns even after the hottest days of summer. These conditions are perfect for creating the high sugars, complex flavors, and high acids that make for great wines.

In the 1970s, Jim Holmes, of then-fledgling Kiona Vineyards, took a good look at the mountain's soils and decided they had just the right consistency for wine grapes. Before long, Kiona had gained national attention with its wines made from Red Mountain grapes, and other wineries, both nearby and elsewhere in the region, soon were competing for their share of those grapes. In April 2001, the Bureau of Alcohol, Tobacco and Firearms agreed that Red Mountain is indeed special and authorized the new Red Mountain AVA. At a mere 3,400 acres, Red Mountain is the smallest of the Washington State appellations.

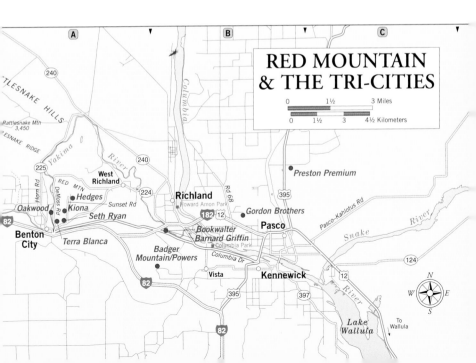

Harvesting merlot grapes atop Red Mountain.

With the neighboring Yakima Valley and Walla Walla Valley AVAs, Red Mountain is part of the vast Columbia Valley AVA—a grab bag of actual and potential vineyard land stretching from Lake Roosevelt in the north across the Columbia River into Oregon. But the outstanding reputation of Red Mountain wines allows winemakers who label their products Red Mountain to ask higher prices.

The bunchgrass and sagebrush uplands of Red Mountain are perhaps the best area in the state for watching and hearing curlews during the summer breeding season. Keep a lookout also for red-tailed hawks, Swainson's hawks, burrowing owls, chukars, mourning doves, rock wrens, and loggerhead shrikes. Coyotes are very common on Red Mountain—they've been known to help themselves to grapes.

Several parks, some of them not quite finished, allow access to the Yakima River and provide picnic spots. (Of course, you can also picnic at the wineries.) The **Tapteal Greenway,** when it's finished, will run for some 30 miles along the lower Yakima River, from Bateman Island in Richland upriver to Benton City; at present, you can picnic where the road touches the river. **Horn Rapids Park,** on the north shore of the river, lies 6 miles north of Benton City on Route 225. It's largely undeveloped, except for a boat ramp near its downstream end. The park has one of

Terra Blanca Vintners is a relative newcomer among Red Mountain wineries.

the region's favorite fishing holes (famed for its big catfish), even though the river level drops considerably in summer. (Bathing here is discouraged, due to recent high levels of pollution from agricultural, chemical, and dairy-farm runoff.) Just downstream, at **Wanawish Dam,** on the fishing platforms that jut out into the Yakima River, fishermen dip their nets to snag migrating salmon.

■ BENTON CITY WINERIES

All the Red Mountain vineyards are within a short drive of one another. To reach them, leave the I-82 freeway at Kiona (Exit 96), a riverside hamlet that once was an important watering place for Horse Heaven Hill ranchers, who drove there with eight-horse teams hauling 500-gallon water tanks. Turn right onto Route 224 before you reach the Yakima River bridge; then turn left onto well-marked DeMoss Road and follow the riverbank to reach Terra Blanca Vintners. (You can also reach the Red Mountain wineries from the Tri-Cities via Route 224.) Drive slowly. The winery is up a steep gravel driveway, overlooking the tiny town of Benton City and the swift-flowing Yakima River—all but hidden beneath trees.

Terra Blanca Vintners *map page 159, A-2*

Terra Blanca is the most exciting winery on Red Mountain. Owner and wine-maker Keith Pilgrim, who is also a geologist, looked far and wide for the perfect soil—high in calcium carbonate, which gives the grapes an earthy flavor, and high in acid, which helps them to develop complexity—and he found it at the future site of Terra Blanca. Construction began in 1993, and the first vines—cabernet sauvignon, merlot, syrah, and chardonnay—were planted a year later. Pilgrim prides himself on the intense flavors of his estate-grown grapes, but his early bottlings (made from purchased grapes) were almost too severely concentrated. More recent bottlings from his own grapes have softened these harsh flavors without sacrificing complexity and intensity. Terra Blanca has one feature most other Washington wineries lack: caves for aging red wines. These are not natural caves, which would be too difficult to create in the sandy, porous volcanic soils. Pilgrim calls them "cut-and-cover caves": two open trenches dug some 400 feet into the mountain, stabilized with precast concrete arches set into place by a large forklift, and then covered over with tons of dirt excavated from the trenches. Each cave is nearly 200 feet long and more than 12 feet wide, with some 2,500 square feet of storage space—room for a thousand small French oak barrels in each one. The caves provide stable year-round temperature and humidity, which makes aging and storing wines much less expensive in this age of rising energy costs. Besides cabernet sauvignon, merlot, and syrah, Terra Blanca has also produced chardonnay, gewürztraminer, and Riesling. *34715 North DeMoss Road; 509-588-6082. Open daily, mid-Feb.–late Dec.*

Oakwood Cellars is tucked into a steep bank above the Yakima River, a short distance north of Terra Blanca on North DeMoss Road.

Oakwood Cellars *map page 159, A-2*

Founded in 1986, this winery is so small, and looks so much like the detached outbuilding of a farm, that you'll miss it if you blink. But it could hardly be in a prettier place—especially in spring, when the wildflowers bloom on the dry slopes above the winery. For such a tiny concern, Oakwood produces some big, impressive wines, and while it's recognized for its cabernet sauvignon, merlot, and lemberger, it has also produced enjoyable chardonnay, sémillon, Riesling, and muscat. The winery's picnic area looks north toward Rattlesnake Mountain, the haunt of hawks and golden eagles. *40504 North DeMoss Road; 509-588-5332. Open Thurs.-Sun., Feb.–Nov.*

The style is largely low-tech and easygoing in the Red Mountain wine region.

To reach the next three wineries, return to Route 224 and turn left (east). Look for the sign directing you to Sunset Road and turn left (north) onto it. You'll immediately come upon the first winery on your left.

Seth Ryan Winery *map page 159, A-2*

Snobs may tell you that wines from this small winery aren't on a par with other Red Mountain wines, perhaps because of a signature pink named Rapture and described by the owners as "rapture in a glass." But Seth Ryan has had a loyal following since it first opened in 1986, making primarily gewürztraminer and Riesling, along with the occasional red. The winery is still small enough for a visitor to be greeted by the winemaker or another of the owners, all of whom are delighted to pour wines and answer questions. At the tasting room you can pick up cheese and other wine-friendly foods to enjoy in the picnic area, which is surrounded by vineyards. *35306 Sunset Road, Benton City; 509-588-6780. Open Thurs.–Mon.*

Continue along Sunset Road, and after a few additional miles, you'll find yourself at Kiona Vineyards.

Kiona Vineyards *map page 159, A-2*

The earliest of the Red Mountain outfits to attract widespread attention, Kiona Vineyards is a small estate winery owned and operated by the John Williams family, which pioneered the Red Mountain viticultural area in the 1970s. This was the first winery to make a distinguished red from lemberger, a lesser German and Austrian grape variety. Kiona's big chardonnays have a following, as do its many late-harvest wines. Lately, though, it has been doing its best work as a grower of grapes. The wines are still of good quality, but some of the recent bottlings haven't been as deep and complex as wines made from Red Mountain grapes by nearby wineries or, for that matter, earlier Kiona vintages. *44612 North Sunset Road; 509-588-6716. Open daily.*

Still farther up the road, on a westward-looking slope, stands the main building of Hedges Cellars.

Hedges Cellars *map page 159, A-2*

Hedges Cellars stands on 75 acres of manicured estate vineyards planted to Bordeaux grape varieties. Completed in 1995, the château-style winery is a bit of an anomaly among the rustic no-frills buildings that dot the landscape. Hedges produces cabernet sauvignon, merlot, cabernet franc, Bordeaux blends, and a sauvignon blanc–chardonnay blend. It was augmented in 1997 by a companion facility, in Issaquah, which has a satellite tasting room, a dining room and professional kitchen, and offices. *53511 North Sunset Road; 509-588-3155. Open Fri.– Sun., Apr.–Dec.*

Currently Red Mountain has no hotels or restaurants, but the lower Yakima Valley and the Tri-Cities are just minutes away via I-82.

Packing wine at the Columbia Valley's Barnard Griffin winery.

COLUMBIA VALLEY
AND THE TRI-CITIES

PERHAPS THE MOST CURIOUS THING about the Columbia Valley—the vast region stretching from the Cascade Mountains east to the Palouse Hills, and from Washington's Okanogan Highlands south to Oregon's Ochocos—is that it's both a basin and a plateau. This geologic anomaly came about because the area had its origin, millions of years ago, as an elevated lava plateau; some of the lava drained away while the remainder, in layers thousands of feet thick, depressed the center with its enormous weight. The basin's high edges rise, mountainlike, at its northern and western rims—forcing the Columbia River to make a long detour to the west as it runs along the basin's northern rim before flowing south again. From a height of more than 2,600 feet above sea level in the north, the plateau slopes to less than 500 feet in the Pasco Basin, where the Columbia forces its way through the Horse Heaven Hills at the Wallula Gap. (If you find it confusing that the Columbia Basin and the Columbia Plateau are, in fact, the same geographic feature, take heart from the fact that the locals do too.)

Add to this odd configuration another immense geologic event: the Ice Age floods that sent enormous quantities of water rushing from a lake in western Montana over the rim of the plateau. The water eroded the basalt into deep coulees and scablands, and it left behind thick deposits of quick-draining, fertile silts, sands, and gravels—the perfect soils for growing grapes.

But grapes need water, and because the region lies in the rain shadow of the Cascades, it's quite dry. Some areas get as little as 6 inches of precipitation annually. What's more, the Columbia Valley lies inland, away from any cooling ocean breezes, and so it's often scorching here in summer. Winters, on the other hand, can be extremely cold, and even at the height of summer the temperatures drop considerably overnight.

Irrigation proved difficult at first, because the Columbia River flows mostly through deep canyons far below the surface of the arable land, and water has to be pumped up the cliffs before it can be guided to the fields. The city of Kennewick began as an agricultural settlement in the late 1880s, thanks to an irrigation canal that brought water from the river to the fields. In the early 1900s, Kennewick had the largest single Concord grape vineyard in the world, but what the city really prided itself on was its strawberries, the earliest to ripen in the state. Agricultural progress wasn't always easy. The canal kept breaking. Wild horses from the Horse

Cabernet sauvignon grows well in the warmer parts of the Columbia Valley.

Heaven Hills invaded the vineyards and fields. After the settlers killed off the coy otes, jackrabbits multiplied enormously and destroyed crops. Growth was slo even after the Hanford Nuclear Reservation, initiated in nearby Richland in 194 gave the area an economic boost.

But salvation was nigh. In the 1930s, visionaries had devised a scheme to build huge dam on the upper Columbia that could generate enough power to pump th river's water over the Columbia Basin's northern rim, after which gravity woul pull it through natural and artificial channels to yet-to-be-established farms. B 1941, the dam, Grand Coulee, then the world's largest concrete structure, was fir ished; construction of the powerhouses and the pumping plant, temporarily halte during World War II, was completed in 1951, and the first water was delivered t the Banks Lake equalizing reservoir.

That year, 66,000 acres were irrigated. In 1973 the pumping was extended the south, and by 1983 four more pump-generator units were installed and opera ing. Because of that water, the area between Kiona Gap, Wallula Gap, Ice Harbo Dam, and the channeled scablands south of Moses Lake is now an agricultural pa adise—and the largest producer of premium wine grapes in Washington.

Once the American wine revolution began, in the 1960s, it didn't take local grapegrowers long to figure out that the Columbia Valley's well-drained soils, hot days, cool nights, and ample irrigation water made the area perfect for vineyards. The sun put fruit and sugar into the grapes, and the cool nights helped them keep their all-important acids (which are quick to dissipate, making for flat wines, in the heat of other hot growing regions, like California's Central Valley). The most important farm, Sagemoor Vineyards, was established in 1968, on the banks of the Columbia River north of Pasco, to produce quality tree fruits and premium wine grapes. The grapes from Sagemoor's Bacchus and Dionysus vineyards turned out to be even better than expected—so good, in fact, that most of Washington State's premium wineries, as well as some Oregon ones, now use them to make their wines.

Other vineyards soon sprang up throughout the Pasco Basin, as well as on the Mattawa and Royal Slopes farther north and on Canoe Ridge (in the Horse Heaven Hills). This proliferation created something of a quandary for wineries with vineyards of their own in the premium growing regions of Red Mountain and the Walla Walla and Yakima Valleys. (These smaller appellations are all contained within the vast Columbia Valley and, depending on the origin of the grapes, wineries can label their wines with either designation.) Columbia Valley grapes yield such wonderful wine that it was often easier for wineries to buy those grapes (or juice from them) than to use their own, which were more expensive to produce and not always as good. Which is why nowadays the Columbia Valley designation shows up on the labels of many premium Walla Walla Valley, Yakima Valley, and Red Mountain wineries.

The ready supply of first-class grapes also led to another anomaly: the creation of wineries in the Puget Sound region that (with a few token vineyards of their own to establish legitimacy) buy most of their grapes (or must, the unfermented juice) in the Columbia Valley and ship them to their wineries west of the Cascades. The state's two largest wineries, Columbia and Chateau Ste. Michelle, have gone a step further, by moving their production facilities east—Columbia to Sunnyside in the Yakima Valley, Chateau Ste. Michelle to its Columbia Crest Winery and to Canoe Ridge, south of the Tri-Cities—while retaining their tasting rooms and visitor facilities in Woodinville, outside Seattle.

The potential for Columbia Valley vineyards seems limitless, since so few of this region's soils and microclimates have been explored fully. Because it contains a great variety of climates and microclimates, from hot to cool, an extraordinary

variety of grapes can be cultivated. The region produces not only excellent reds, like barbera, cabernet sauvignon, cabernet franc, malbec, merlot, nebbiolo, petite sirah, petit verdot, sangiovese, syrah, and zinfandel (and some interesting lemberger), but also superb whites, like chardonnay, marsanne, muscat, rousanne, sauvignon blanc, sémillon, viognier, and, in cooler vineyards, gewürztraminer, chenin blanc, pinot gris, and Riesling.

The first aficionados of Columbia Valley grapes arrived some years before the wine boom. During World War II, Italian prisoners of war in a camp near Pasco worked in Fred Pardini's Richland vineyard and appreciated both his grapes and his homemade zinfandel. Apparently the POW camp lacked walls and fences, and prisoners were allowed to make "field trips" into Pasco and Kennewick to break up the monotony of internment.

Kennewick, Pasco, and Richland—known collectively as the Tri-Cities—grew from tiny farming towns into major cities as the Hanford Nuclear Reservation grew in size. But they haven't suffered that much from the Reservation's decline. New industries have moved in, augmenting agriculture and viticulture. The **Pasco Farmers Market** is the state's largest farmers' market, with a truly amazing selection of locally grown or made products. *104 South Fourth Avenue (at Columbia Street), Pasco; 509-545-0738. Wed. and Sat., 8–noon, May–Nov.*

While the Tri-Cities have only a handful of wineries, Pasco has an important regional airport, and lodgings in Pasco, Richland, and Kennewick are within easy driving distance of Red Mountain, Yakima Valley, and Walla Walla Valley wineries. The nicest hotels border the west bank of the Columbia River in Richland, north of I-182, with easy access to Howard Amon Park and the riverfront path: **Hampton Inn** (486 Bradley Boulevard, Richland; 509-943-4400); **Red Lion Richland Hanford House** (802 George Washington Way, Richland; 509-946-7611); and **Shilo Inn** (50 Comstock Street, Richland; 509-946-4661). Restaurants and shopping are nearby, on and off George Washington Way.

Local favorites among the region's many restaurants include the **Blue Moon** (20 North Auburn, Kennewick; 509-582-6598), with its formal dining room and seven-course meals on Fridays and Saturdays; **Atomic Ale Brewpub & Eatery** (1015 Lee Boulevard, Richland; 509-946-5465), with good microbrews and pub food; **Henry's** (1435 George Washington Way, Richland; 509-946-8706), popular for its steaks, seafood, and pastas; **Rattlesnake Mountain Brewing Company** (2696 North Columbia Center Boulevard, Richland; 509-783-5747), with fine

views of the river and the eponymous mountains; **Casa Chapala** (107 East Columbia Drive, Kennewick; 509-582-7848), a friendly Mexican family restaurant; and the comfortable **Samovar Russian Fine Dining & Bakery** (1340 Jadwin, Richland; 509-946-6655).

The Columbia Valley has more to offer visitors than wine and wineries. The region includes three beautiful lakes—Chelan, Roosevelt, and Moses—as well as the Grand Coulee and the Yakima River Canyon. The lakes, marshes, rivers, and creeks support an incredible variety of wildlife. Three rivers—the Columbia, the Yakima, and the Snake—are the Tri-Cities' major attraction. The miles of riverfront parks and trails in Richland and Kennewick are lovely oases on warm evenings.

Howard Amon Park, which winds along the Columbia waterfront in Richland, is pretty all year, with shady lawns and riverside trees alive with birdsong, but it's truly spectacular in autumn, when the foliage of the ginkgo trees planted along the levee turns golden. Kennewick's **Columbia Park** is a vast, grassy playground stretching along the river for about 3 miles. (The skeleton of Kennewick Man

(opposite) Vendors sell produce and other items at the large open-air Pasco Farmers Market.
(above) Howard Amon Park in Richland.

turned up here in 1996.) **Two Rivers Park,** 2 miles east of Kennewick near the community of Finley, has 16 acres at its west end for picnicking and swimming; the east end has a boat-launching ramp, docks, and parking. **Hover Park,** on the Columbia River approximately 10 miles southeast of Kennewick, is currently undeveloped but occupies a site on a protected lagoon. The Longmire Wagon Train, the first to pass through the area, crossed the Columbia River on rafts near the current park site in 1853.

Unfortunately, the Columbia Valley is subject to dangerous dust storms—especially along I-82, I-182, U.S. 395, and Route 240 in the Tri-Cities area. Rising suddenly, strong winds can kick up enough dust to reduce visibility to zero, which in turn causes numerous automobile accidents. It's wise to wait out a dust storm at a winery, restaurant, or riverfront park.

■ TRI-CITIES WINERIES

Several Tri-Cities wineries are among the most important in the state, and they're also fun places to visit. All are within easy driving distances of one another and are close to major hotels. Two of the most important, Bookwalter and Barnard Griffin, are right off I-182 as it enters the Tri-Cities from the west—yet they're both surprisingly secluded, on a vineyard-clad slope. They stand next to each other on a short country lane. Approaching on I-182, take Exit 3A (Queensgate Road) and turn south towards Columbia Park Trail, turning onto it shortly (after a third of a mile). After a similarly short distance, turn left onto Windmill Road, then right, almost immediately, onto Tulip Lane. Bookwalter Winery is up the hill.

■ RICHLAND

Bookwalter Winery *map page 159, B-2*

Established in 1983 by Jerry Bookwalter, a former general manager of Sagemoor Farms, which pioneered the cultivation of wine grapes in the Columbia Valley, Bookwalter Winery has switched its emphasis from light wines—quaffable chenin blancs and Rieslings—to serious, more complex ones. Zelma Long, who made her mark as the winemaker at California's Simi Winery, was brought on board as a consultant in 2000, and Bookwalter now has a following for its rich cabernet sauvignons. The winery looks like an office building or a medical complex, but don't let that put you off. The wines made here are worth

seeking out, and the "tasting lounge" is a relaxing place to linger. *894 Tulip Lane; 509-627-5000. Open daily.*

The small Barnard Griffin winery is just up the lane from Bookwalter.

Barnard Griffin *map page 159, B-2*

Veteran winemaker Rob Griffin, formerly of Preston and Hogue, founded this winery in 1983 with—as its name reflects—his wife, Deborah Barnard. Their wines have long been among the best in the state and still offer terrific value. But the last few vintages have seen a change in emphasis. The regular wines have become lighter and less complex—but the reserve wines, fermented in small barrels and aged in oak, rank among Washington's finest. Barnard Griffin's best wines are chardonnay, fumé blanc, sémillon, merlot, and cabernet sauvignon. Library and special-release wines are available only at the winery. *878 Tulip Lane; 509-627-0266. Open daily.*

Barnard Griffin produces many fine wines but is best known for chardonnay, fumé blanc, sémillon, merlot, and cabernet sauvignon.

Badger Mountain has proven that great wines can be made from organically grown grapes.

■ **KENNEWICK**

The next winery sits in the shade on a south-facing slope of Badger Mountain, at the far end of a Kennewick housing subdivision. It's a bit trickier to find. From I-82, take Exit 109 and turn north onto Clearwater Avenue; then, after a quarter mile, turn left (west) onto Leslie Road, which curves north. After another quarter mile, turn left onto Rachel Road (which also curves north); follow it for about a mile to Clover Road, and turn left. At Jurupa Street turn right. The winery is about a quarter mile past the last turn; signs will direct you.

Badger Mountain/Powers Winery *map page 159, B-2*

Badger Mountain, the first certified-organic vineyard in Washington State to make estate wines, has proved that it's possible to make great organic wines—if you have the right grapes. The winery produces several reds from Bordeaux grape varieties, as well as no-added-sulfite chardonnay and Riesling. Powers Winery, which occupies the same facility, has gained a following for its reasonably priced, consistently high-quality reds, which include a fine lemberger, a complex cabernet sauvignon, a very good syrah, a cabernet sauvignon–merlot blend, and a proprietary red blend (cabernet sauvignon, merlot, and cabernet franc) called Parallel 46. Among the several whites are a chardonnay, a pinot gris, and a sauvignon blanc. *1106 South Jurupa Street, Kennewick; 509-627-4986. Open daily; tours by appointment.*

Backtrack east on Clover and Rachel Roads; turn left (north) onto Leslie Road. After 2.5 miles, turn right onto Columbia Park Trail; then, after three quarters of a mile, turn left onto Route 240W (towards Richland). After about 1.75 miles, merge east onto I-182E/U.S. 12E (toward Pasco). After crossing the Columbia River, take Exit 9, to Road 68, which you'll reach in 3 miles; turn left (north) onto Road 68. After half a mile, turn right onto Burden Boulevard. Gordon Brothers comes up on the right after three quarters of a mile; watch for signs.

■ **PASCO**

Gordon Brothers Family Vineyards *map page 159, B-2*

In 1980, Jeff and Bill Gordon and their families began planting a 90-acre vineyard on a perfectly oriented south-facing slope above the north bank of the Snake River, 2 miles north of Ice Harbor Dam. When they began to release wines, they had a small tasting room in Jeff Gordon's home, which overlooks the vineyard—a delightful arrangement, but despite its scenic setting, a bit too far off the beaten path to attract any but the most determined visitors. So in 1996 the Gordon brothers built themselves a new winery and tasting room closer to town. It's right next door to a major sports complex and convention center and it backs onto a subdivision, but visitors to the tasting room are in for a surprise: none of these distractions are visible from the large windows, which look south across vineyards to the distant Horse Heaven Hills. Instantly you forget the urban setting. The wines are so good they don't need a boost from the scenery. Gordon Brothers sells some of its grapes to other wineries but reserve about 45 percent to produce almost 10,000 cases of chardonnay, cabernet sauvignon, merlot, and limited-edition Tradition, a blend of cabernet and merlot. In the 1990s, the merlot attracted a cult following, but the cabernet is every bit as good. *5960 Burden Boulevard; 509-547-6331. Open daily.*

The oldest established winery in the Tri-Cities sits on a low vineyard slope several miles north of Pasco. To get there, return to I-182 by way of Burden Boulevard and Road 68. Turn left (east) onto I-182 E/U.S. 12E. After passing through Pasco (about 6 miles), merge north onto U.S. 395 (toward Spokane) and continue for about 5 miles. Turn right onto East Vineyard Drive and follow the signs to Preston Premium Wines, which you can see from U.S. 395.

Preston Premium Wines *map page 159, B-1*

Bill Preston, who died in 2001, was one of the pioneers of the 1970s Washington wine boom, and his family carries on his tradition. The Prestons first planted a 50-acre vineyard in 1972. It has grown to 171 acres, putting the family among the largest growers in the Columbia Valley. Preston has produced wines of its own from these estate grapes since 1976, and while it's best known for its merlot and cabernet sauvignon, it also produces splendid chardonnay, as well as a little sparking wine and port. The winery offers an excellent self-guided tour. Close by is an attractive picnic area, with a pond, a gazebo, and an amphitheater. *502 East Vineyard Drive; 509-545-1990. Open daily.*

(opposite, and following spread) The Walla Walla Valley has emerged as Washington's premier viticultural region. (Brent Bergherm)

WALLA WALLA VALLEY

An engraving of a Nez Perce camp, made in 1853 by John Mix Stanley.

SHIELDED FROM THE COLD NORTHEAST WINDS by the rolling hills of the Palouse and by spurs of the Blue Mountains, yet open to the sea breezes blowing up the Columbia River, the Walla Walla Valley occupies a unique position in eastern Washington. Its growing season resembles those of many western Washington valleys, its porous soils (whether sandy or gravelly) are friendly to vines, and its warm summer days pack flavor into the grapes. No wonder the Walla Walla Valley has emerged as Washington's premier viticultural region. Alas, demand and prices have kept pace with fame, and Walla Walla wines can be difficult to find outside the valley. But new wineries are springing up each year.

The Walla Walla Valley is only 50 miles (an hour-and-a-half drive) east of the Tri-Cities via U.S. 12—for much of the trip, a two-lane highway.

■ WEST OF WALLA WALLA

Driving east from the Tri-Cities on U.S. 12, a short distance south of the Snake River crossing, signs direct you to the **McNary National Wildlife Refuge** (64 Maple Road, Burbank; 509-547-4942). The marshes, sloughs, and upland meadows of the refuge are most enjoyable in spring and summer, after the hunters have left. A self-guided 2-mile trail winds through the marshes, and a blind (built like a small cabin) hidden in the tall reeds allows visitors to watch ducks, geese, grebes, and yellow-headed blackbirds up close. Farther on, the town of **Wallula** was the first place Western Civilization touched this region. Lewis and Clark camped here in 1806; the Wilkes Expedition passed through in 1841; and explorer John C. Frémont camped here in 1843. But, more important, David Thompson, a fur trader of the Northwest Company, claimed the region for Great Britain in 1811 and built Fort Nez Perce—later known as Fort Walla Walla—to support the claim. The fort now lies beneath the waters of Lake Wallula.

A few miles farther on, U.S. 12 turns inland alongside the Walla Walla River. If you have time for a diversion, continue along the Columbia on Route 730 for 2 more miles, and watch for the **Twin Sisters,** a double-towered basalt formation on the left, and turn into the small gravel parking lot. The 800-foot-tall basalt cliffs along the Columbia River are part of the **Wallula Gap,** the cleft the Columbia River cut through the Horse Heaven Hills on its way to the sea, that, some 12,000 years ago, the Spokane Floods widened. Come spring, the roadside cliffs are dotted with wildflowers.

U.S. 12 soon veers away from the green banks of the Walla Walla River and crosses a series of ridges with basalt outcroppings. The Spokane Floods deposited the silty soil that covers the basalt. A few miles farther on, the highway drops down to the green floor of the Walla Walla Valley. Long famous for asparagus, sweet onions, cherries, and wheat, the valley has recently evolved into one of America's premier wine regions. The farther east from the rain shadow of the Cascade Mountains you travel, the more lush the landscape becomes. (Yakima and Richland receive only about 6 inches of rain a year; Walla Walla's annual rainfall averages 20 inches).

The roadside wheat hamlet of **Touchet** (pronounced "TOO-shee"), the first set-tlement on this route, has one important asset that can be hard to find around here: a gas station. A few miles farther east, tall grain elevators mark **Lowden,** another wheat-growing hamlet. Lowden has the look of hard times; the sagging fronts of abandoned shops line the north side of the main thoroughfare. But two local wineries have recently earned the town its share of renown. Both are on the left (north) side of the highway.

Woodward Canyon Winery *map page 185, A-3*

Woodward Canyon Winery occupies a seemingly incongruous place: a modest building behind the Small family's grain elevator and machine shop. But this little winery has become a place of pilgrimage for enophiles, who make the trip for the superb cabernet sauvignon, merlot, and chardonnay (and, occasionally, other varieties). Winemaker Rick Small divides his time between winemaking and marketing, and he's often at the winery. The Smalls recently moved their tasting room into a restored house next door, almost in L'Ecole No. 41's front yard. Now, for the first time, the winery looks almost elegant. *11920 West Highway 12, Lowden; 509-525-4129. Open daily.*

Just a barrel toss farther east, on the same side of the highway, look for the sign directing you to L'Ecole No. 41.

L'Ecole No. 41 *map page 185, A-3*

Nearly everyone loves this laid-back winery, housed in the cellars of Lowden's 1915 Frenchtown school. A lightheartedness prevails here, expressed in the children's' artwork on the winery's labels and in the listing of wines on an old blackboard—pleasant touches that too many "serious" wineries lack. But there's nothing lighthearted about the quality of the wines, which L'Ecole has been turning out since 1983 and which rank among the valley's very best. In recent years, the sémillon and merlot have been particularly outstanding. *41 Lowden School Road, Lowden; 509-525-0940. Open daily, but call ahead during winter.*

As you continue up the valley, look for a big rock on the south side of the highway, about 7 miles past Lowden, marking the entrance to Three Rivers Winery.

Three Rivers Winery *map page 185, A-3*

Atop a small knoll overlooking the surrounding vineyards, Three Rivers has excellent views of Mill Creek, the historic Whitman Mission site, and the Walla Walla Valley beyond; on clear days, you can see all the way to the Blue Mountains to the east and southeast. Wines made here include merlot, cabernet sauvignon, syrah, and sangiovese, as well as a cabernet-merlot blend. Three Rivers is a nicely appointed facility that wouldn't look out of place in California's Napa or Sonoma Valleys. It also has a unique feature: the winery entertains visitors with a three-hole golf course. *5641 West Highway 12, Walla Walla; 509-526-9463. Open daily.*

Just beyond Three Rivers, south of the highway and 7 miles west of Walla Walla, is one of the state's most important historic sites. The **Whitman Mission National Historic Site** preserves the site of Waiilatpu Mission, the Presbyterian mission that Marcus and Narcissa Whitman established on Cayuse Indian lands in 1836. For 11 years, the mission was a vital stop for pioneers on the Oregon Trail; you can still see some of the ruts their wagon wheels made. But in November 1847, after an outbreak of measles left half the Cayuse tribe dead, angry Cayuse warriors, who blamed the Americans for the epidemic, destroyed the mission, killing the Whitmans and 11 others.

The other **Fort Walla Walla**—the one built by the U.S. Army in 1857 to replace the old fort at Wallula—is one of 12 historic buildings or replicas transported or built here to celebrate the area's pioneer heritage. The on-site museum contains 35,000 or so artifacts and other materials. *755 Myra Road; 509-525-7703.*

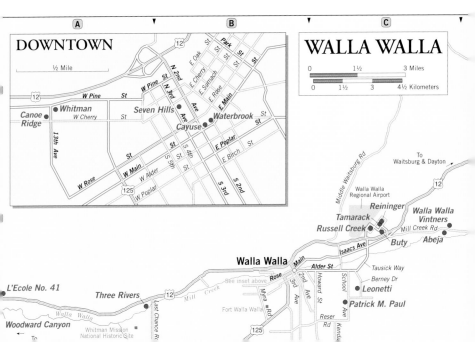

■ DOWNTOWN WALLA WALLA

Walla Walla is the valley's undisputed metropolis. By the late 1800s it was the largest city in Washington Territory. And it was an early hotbed of wine-grape cultivation. One of the most successful local nurserymen was Philip Ritz, who planted 21 varieties of grapes in 1863. ("Prospects" of Walla Walla—a series of panoramic engravings published during the last decades of the 19th century—document Ritz's rising wealth. An 1860s prospect depicts a humble farmhouse surrounded by orchards and vineyards; by the 1880s, there's a mansion, complete with carriage drive, in a parklike setting.) By 1865, Frank Orselli, an Italian immigrant, was growing grapes and retailing wine in Walla Walla. In the 1870s, Jean Marie Abadie was producing 400 gallons of white wine and 150 gallons of red wine annually—but we don't have any record of how it tasted. In December 1890, "In the Crescent of the Blue Mountains," an article in the *Overland Monthly and Out West Magazine*, described the Walla Walla Valley as having "a soil unsurpassed for grain field and garden, for orchard and vineyard,"—a description that still holds true today.

Downtown Walla Walla has escaped the blight of fast-food joints and warehouse stores.

Walla Walla got its start as an important Indian camp site, and even today its streets, instead of aligning with the compass points, flow off from the ancient Nez Perce Trail that became Main Street. The town has escaped much of the blight of fast-food joints and warehouse stores, and there's little suburban sprawl: the transition from city to farmland occurs with surprising suddenness. By the time you approach Walla Walla, U.S. 12 has blossomed into a freeway; Second Street whisks you from it so quickly that you'll probably miss the watchtowers and razor-wire fences of the state penitentiary at the northwestern outskirts of town. (In fact, you'll hardly hear the place mentioned: Walla Walla has cultivated an image of a farm-and-college town so successfully that most visitors are unaware of the prison.)

Walla Walla has gone to great lengths to preserve its architectural history. The heart of downtown, at Second and Main, looks pretty much as it did a century ago, with many old buildings beautifully maintained and with newer structures designed to fit in. Much of the area underwent a sprucing-up in 1992, and in 1994 the city launched a project "to help preserve Walla Walla's rich architectural and cultural history" by encouraging people throughout the community to honor historical buildings through restoration and identification with historical markers.

Judging from the great number of well-preserved buildings, many with plaques, the plan is working. Recent triumphs include the restoration of **Naimy's Furniture Building** (200 East Main Street), and of the **Whitehouse-Crawford Planing Mill** (212 North Third Street) by Seven Hills Winery. Among other downtown buildings of interest is the 1917 **Liberty Theatre** (50 East Main Street), which rises above the spot where Steptoe's Fort stood in the 1850s. The theater's exterior was restored in the early 1990s; the interior is now part of a department store.

Just past the intersection of Second and Main stands **Die Brücke** (1903), also known as the Bridge Building, so named because it bridges Mill Creek. (You can see a short stretch of Mill Creek "exposed" diagonally across Main Street, near the Waterbrook Tasting Room.) Washington State's first Constitutional Convention took place on the second floor of the 1878 **Reynolds-Day Building** (6 East Main Street), in a room known as Science Hall. The **Paine Building** (1879), at the corner of Main and Second Streets, is decorated with striking geometric patterns. The **Baker Boyer Building,** also at this corner, is home to Washington's oldest operating commercial bank.

Farther west, Canoe Ridge Vineyards helped rejuvenate Walla Walla's former railroad and red-light district by opening its winery and tasting room in the engine house of the old Walla Walla street car company, near the intersection of West

Cherry and North 13th Streets, and by erecting a new, bigger winery building to the west. In 2002, Christophe Baron, the owner and winemaker of Cayuse Vineyards, bought a former bordello on the corner of West Main Street and Fourth Avenue and set about turning it and a neighboring building into a working winery, complete with tasting room and professional kitchen.

More than the presence of historic buildings has kept downtown Walla Walla alive. It's an exceptionally people-friendly area where both residents and visitors love to shop, eat, and check out wineries. The **Walla Walla Farmers Market,** held on Saturdays from mid-May to mid-October in **Crawford Park** (Fourth and Main Streets), is shielded from the summer sun by a shady arcade.

The city has several good restaurants, of which the most popular is **Merchants Ltd.** (21 East Main Street; 509-525-0900), a classic deli and bakery, which serves inexpensive breakfasts and lunches six days a week and gets jammed on Saturdays. The selection of local wines is superb. The **Whitehouse-Crawford Restaurant** (55 West Cherry Street; 509-525-2222) opened in 2001—in the same restored brick building as Seven Hills Winery—to great acclaim. The chef prepares seasonal dishes and makes the most out of local white asparagus and morels. This restaurant also has an extensive Walla Walla Valley wine list.

The **Marcus Whitman Hotel** (6 West Rose Street; 509-525-2200 or 866-826-9422), built in 1928 and recently restored and upgraded, has become the crown jewel of downtown Walla Walla.

Driving in from the west, the first of downtown Walla Walla's several noteworthy wineries is Canoe Ridge.

Canoe Ridge Vineyard *map page 185, B-2*

Canoe Ridge created a stir a few years back, because it marked the first foray of its parent company, California's Chalone Group, into the Pacific Northwest. Once Chalone planted vineyards at Canoe Ridge, above the Columbia River, other wineries quickly followed suit. But Chalone, acting on a hunch, put the winery itself in Walla Walla, and the hunch paid off: the facility, in an old engine house, has become one of Washington's premier wine destinations. Once you taste the luscious merlot, with undertones of raspberry, cherry, and chocolate, or the big, buttery chardonnay, or the crisp and spicy gewürztraminer, you'll know why.

(opposite) Harvested grapes at Canoe Ridge Vineyards. (following spread) John Abbott, of Abeja, hovers over the winepress.

The Whitehouse-Crawford building in Walla Walla is now home to Seven Hills Winery.

A large (and very pink) barrel house west of the engine house has 10-inch-thick concrete walls, with a 4-inch-thick layer of insulation sandwiched in the middle—sufficient to keep any wine at an even temperature on the coldest winter night or the hottest summer day. Longtime winemaker John Abbot retired in 2002 to start a winery of his own (see Abeja, on page 201), but, happily, the quality of Canoe Ridge has not suffered for the change. The new winemaker is Kendall Mix. *1102 West Cherry Street; 509-527-0885. Open daily.*

Whitman Cellars *map page 185, B-2*

Whitman Cellars, not far from Canoe Ridge, is a winery worth watching. It uses only handpicked cabernet sauvignon, merlot, syrah, and viognier grapes from area vineyards, which it ages in French, Hungarian, and American oak. Before Whitman opened its new winery and tasting room, its wines were made at other area wineries; but even now, with a facility of its own, production of the hand-crafted wines is still limited to small quantities of each variety. *1015 West Pine Street; 509-529-1142. Open Wed.–Sat.*

Seven Hills Winery *map page 185, B-2*

Seven Hills started out in Oregon in 1988, but 12 years later it moved a few miles north to Walla Walla, and the winery now occupies a restored brick building that once housed a planing mill in the heart of downtown. It was a smart move: the wines have gotten much better with the change of states. Seven Hills makes intensely flavored merlot, cabernet sauvignon, and syrah, designed to be laid down and aged for several years, but sufficiently well-balanced, with enough fruit, to be enjoyed while they're still young. To offset these "heavy" offerings, the winery also makes some sprightly pinot gris and Riesling. *212 North Third Avenue; 509-529-7198. Open Tues.–Sat.*

Waterbrook Winery *map page 185, B-2*

Waterbrook, the Valley's largest winery, is hidden away in a converted warehouse just south of Lowden, but the tasting room is in downtown Walla Walla. It's a fun place to visit, because there's always an art exhibit (occasionally wacky) on view. The winery's chardonnay, sauvignon blanc, and viognier are its most popular

Waterbrook Winery's subdued downtown tasting room.

bottlings. Waterbrook is also known for a red blend (sangiovese, syrah, merlot, and cabernet sauvignon) called Mélange, and for its Red Mountain meritage (merlot, cabernet franc, and cabernet sauvignon). During warm weather you can sit outside the tasting room on a brick-paved patio and watch the downtown traffic go by as you sip. *31 East Main Street; 509-522-1262. Open daily.*

Cayuse Vineyards *map page 185, B-2*
When the French vigneron Christophe Baron discovered an old dry riverbed full of cobbles, he knew he'd found the right place for a vineyard—drainage could hardly get much better. Little wonder that the wines his Cayuse Vineyards produces are among the most complex in the valley. The winery's tasting room is in a bright yellow building in downtown Walla Walla (next to Merchants Ltd.). Before Baron bought the narrow-fronted building, it had served as a shoe-repair business; the restoration won him an architectural award. Cayuse wines are so popular that in the spring of 2003 the tasting-room window bore this sign: "Sorry, we are sold out. We look forward to seeing you next fall . . . . Thanks!" *17 East Main Street; 509-526-0686. Call for hours.*

■ SOUTH OF WALLA WALLA

Colvin Vineyards *map page 185, C-3*

Colvin Vineyards makes handcrafted reds and red blends, including cabernet sauvignon, cabernet franc, merlot, syrah, and carmenère, an old Bordeaux grape that's no longer grown in France but that makes a claret in the Walla Walla Valley with a pleasant, spicy undertaste. The winery building was designed by owner and winemaker Mark Colvin and built with local logs (from a tree farm, he's quick to point out) and local stone. Even the logo on the winery's label is derived from a hunk of local rock; Colvin's small daughter found the intricately patterned stone in the vineyards. *4122 Powerline Road; 509-527-9463. Open Sat. and by appointment.*

Isenhower Cellars *map page 185, B-3*

The rustic barn housing Isenhower Cellars blends unobtrusively into the valley's landscape of farms and wheat fields. There are no vineyards, because this is a new winery and the Isenhowers, like many Walla Walla wine entrepreneurs, do not make the bulk of their wines from local grapes, but rather from grapes grown in the nearby Columbia Valley and Red Mountain. The fine Wild Alfalfa syrah, for example, is made with grapes (15 percent cabernet sauvignon to round out the wine) from the Wahluke Slope, Red Mountain, and the Walla Walla Valley. The Isenhowers also produce cabernet sauvignon, merlot, and a rousanne-viognier blend. Owners and co-winemakers Brett and Denise Isenhower are pharmacists, which apparently gave them a leg on up wine chemistry when they decided to start making wine in 1999, first at Glen Fiona, then at Rulo, and now at their own winery. *3471 Pranger Road; 509-526-7896. Open weekends and by appointment.*

Glen Fiona *map page 185, B-3*

Glen Fiona—Gaelic for "Valley of the Vine"—hit a few bumps over the past few years, but with the 2001 opening of a new winery in the middle of a 21-acre estate, and with Caleb Foster now in charge of making the wine, things are looking up. Glen Fiona is unique among local wineries in making wine from only one grape: syrah. Using traditional, low-intervention techniques, Foster ferments the wine in small, open-top vats before aging it in used oak barrels (to limit oak extracts in the finished wine). It's a big, Rhône-style syrah that ages well and, eventually, opens up beautifully. *1249 Lyday Lane (via Braden Road); 509-522-2566. Open Sat. or by appointment.*

Pepper Bridge Winery *map page 185, B-3*

The winery itself is only a few years old, but Pepper Bridge has a long history as a premium Walla Walla grapegrower, with vineyards in the appellation's Oregon portion. An area classic, it has inspired other wineries to set up shop in this region. Pepper Bridge makes only cabernet sauvignon and merlot, from Walla Walla Valley grapes. *1704 J. B. George Road; 509-525-6502. Open Mon.–Sat.*

■ WALLA WALLA AIRPORT WINE GHETTO

A few years ago, someone at the Port of Walla Walla had a bright idea: why not redevelop the desolate area east of the airport, where a few World War II barracks and service buildings had survived decades of neglect, and turn it into a wine center? With young winemakers offered terms so generous they couldn't refuse, the plan worked. Several small wineries are now established here, all so successful that winemakers from other regions now jestingly refer to the compound as the Walla Walla Airport Wine Ghetto. But don't let the place's aesthetics turn you off—close your eyes if you must. As soon as you taste the wines, you're bound to smile.

Buty *map page 185, C-2*

Winemaker Caleb Foster, who put in several years at Woodward Canyon Winery and in New Zealand, and who's also the consulting winemaker for Glen Fiona, produces red wines you'll fall in love with at first sip. Although the funky winery's name is pronounced "beauty" (after the middle name of his wife and partner, Nina Buty Foster), you won't see a lot of beauty in the former barracks that houses the tasting room. Not to worry: the beauty is in the wines—especially a blend of merlot and cabernet franc (with no special name), a blend of cabernet sauvignon and syrah called Rediviva, a blend of cabernet sauvignon and cabernet franc simply labeled Red Table Wine, and a white blend of sémillon and sauvignon blanc. *535 East Cessna Avenue; 509-527-0901. Open daily (with a few exceptions).*

Reininger *map page 185, C-2*

Reininger was the first winery to occupy one of the old World War II buildings near the airport. And it's one of the few Walla Walla wineries to use only grapes grown in the Walla Walla Valley. The results are spectacular. Reininger's cabernet sauvignon is particularly splendid, though its cabernet franc, merlot, and syrah are also so good that the winery is on its way to developing a cult following. *720 C Street; 509-522-1994. Call ahead for hours.*

Christophe Baron, of Cayuse Vineyards, with his syrah grapes.

Russell Creek Winery *map page 185, C-2*

This tiny winery began in 1988 on a small farm nestled in a draw of the Blue Mountains, east of Walla Walla. Starting with just a hand press and 5-gallon carboys (glass bottles), winemaker Larry Krivoshein hand-crafted full-bodied red wines. Success brought a bigger press as well as barrels, and the winery has now moved closer to civilization at the Walla Walla airport. Its merlots are delicious. *301 Aeronca Avenue; 509-386-4401. Open daily.*

Tamarack Cellars *map page 185, C-2*

Tucked into a restored fire station and barracks, this winery produces small lots of first-rate cabernet sauvignon, merlot, and chardonnay, as well as an aptly named Firehouse Red, from grapes grown in the Walla Walla, Yakima, and Columbia Valleys. Production is small (Tamarack produced only 5,800 cases in 2002), because the emphasis is on hand-crafting the wines to extract the most flavor and complexity from the grapes. *700 C Street; 509-526-3533. Open Sat. and by appointment.*

Several additional wineries at the Airport Wine Ghetto are worth visiting: **Dunham Cellars** (150 East Boeing Avenue; 509-529-4685); **Five Star Cellars** (840 C Street; 509-527-8400); and **Cougar Crest Winery** (202 A Street; 509-529-5980). Call for hours.

■ EAST OF WALLA WALLA

Leonetti Cellar *map page 185, C-3*

Leonetti Cellar is the Walla Walla Valley's most famous winery—so famous that it's closed to the public and its wines are almost impossible to obtain. But you can try to get on the mailing list. Or you can check the wine department at Merchants Ltd. in downtown Walla Walla, which sometimes stocks Leonetti wines, including the much-touted reserve—a blend of red Bordeaux varieties, made only from vintages that winemaker Gary Figgins deems worthy. The blends

Wines from Leonetti Cellar are often difficult to obtain.

making up the reserve vary with the vintages, reflecting Figgins's quest to produce "the finest, most hedonistic wine possible, regardless of varietal content." Inventory is minuscule (only 665 cases in 2000). Leonetti also produces merlot and cabernet sauvignon, as well as an elegant, complex sangiovese from Walla Walla Valley grapes. *1875 Foothills Lane. 509-525-1428. Not open to the public.*

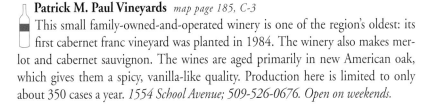

Patrick M. Paul Vineyards *map page 185, C-3*
This small family-owned-and-operated winery is one of the region's oldest: its first cabernet franc vineyard was planted in 1984. The winery also makes merlot and cabernet sauvignon. The wines are aged primarily in new American oak, which gives them a spicy, vanilla-like quality. Production here is limited to only about 350 cases a year. *1554 School Avenue; 509-526-0676. Open on weekends.*

Walla Walla Vintners *map page 185, C-2*
Walla Walla Vintners is another small winery with a limited production of reds: cabernet sauvignon, cabernet franc, merlot, and sangiovese. The wines are made in very small lots and aged in American and French oak. The place is well worth a visit, because these excellent wines are otherwise hard to find. *225 Vineyard Lane (off Mill Creek Road); 509-525-4724. Open Sat. and by appointment.*

Abeja *map page 185, C-2*
John Abbot was the founding winemaker at Canoe Ridge Vineyards; he retired in 2002 to found a winery of his own. He opened Abeja in a century-old farmhouse that stands amid 22 acres of gardens, creek, and vineyards, Abbot now makes cabernet sauvignon and small batches of chardonnay from Walla Walla and Columbia Valley grapes; his first release was in the fall of 2003. He has renamed the guest cottages on the property, formerly known Mill Creek Inn, as the Inn at Abeja (509-522-1234). There's a wildlife habitat nearby. *2014 Mill Creek Road; 509-526-7400. Open by appointment only.*

At present there are few vineyards and wineries farther east of Walla Walla, but that situation could soon change. In April 2003, Michael Murr, a local philanthropist and New York investor, reached a final agreement with the Walla Walla County Commissioners to permit the introduction of a winery into what had been an exclusively agricultural zone southeast of town—after two years of court challenges by local farmers, who wanted no wineries among their wheat fields. Murr has planned his new winery as a showplace for the region, and it may well spawn further vineyard and winery development. It would be difficult to find a more scenic location for wineries anywhere in the West than this corner of the state, where the rolling hills look south and east toward the Blue Mountains.

If the vintners to the southeast win the zoning battle, the area to the northeast might see development as well, and sleepy small towns such as **Waitsburg** could become wine destinations. Waitsburg, 21.5 miles northeast of Walla Walla on U.S. 12, got its start in 1865, when Sylvester M. Wait built a gristmill on the banks of the Touchet River. The town prospered to such an extent that for a time it rivaled Walla Walla for regional dominance. An old business district and several elegant homes from the 1880s bear witness to the town's former glory.

Dayton, 10 miles northeast of Waitsburg on U.S. 12, at the confluence of the Touchet River and Patit Creek, has all the makings of a great vineyard town—gentle hills, ample rainfall, and sufficient heat—and a historic downtown to attract visitors. The county seat of Columbia County, it's worth a stop just to see its 88 Victorian buildings (listed on the National Register of Historic Places), which include the Columbia County Courthouse (1887), the Dayton Depot (1881), and several well-preserved homes from the 1870s and 1880s. A brochure containing two self-guided walking tours is available from the Dayton Chamber of Commerce (166 East Main Street; 509-382-4825). **Patit Creek Restaurant** (725 East Main Street; 509-382-2625) not only serves the area's best meals in the region (glorious beef dishes, legendary huckleberry and raspberry pies) but also has an excellent list of local wines.

As delicious as they are, apples are being replaced by grapes in much of eastern Washington.

PRACTICAL INFORMATION

■ AREA CODES AND TIME ZONE

The area code for Seattle is 206; for Everett and south Snohomish County, Bellevue and east King County, 425; for Olympia and the San Juan Islands, 360; for Tacoma, Puyallup, and the south Puget Sound area, 253; and for Spokane and eastern Washington, 509. The 360 area code shares some territories in western Washington with 564. All of the state is in the Pacific time zone.

■ METRIC CONVERSIONS

1 foot = .305 meters   1 mile = 1.6 kilometers   1 pound = .45 kilograms
Centigrade = Fahrenheit temperature minus 32, divided by 1.8

■ CLIMATE

It rains a *lot* in Washington west of the Cascades, especially from fall through spring, but summers are usually dry and reasonably warm—high temperatures average in the upper 70s Fahrenheit, with nighttime lows in the 50s. Snow rarely falls west of the Cascades, though the region does get the occasional blizzard. Cold spells last a couple of weeks at most, and even during snowy periods daytime temperatures usually rise above freezing. The best times for traveling the lowlands are from mid-March to mid-October, when weather surprises are few.

The wine regions east of the Cascades get much less precipitation, and some of what they do get comes in the form of snow. Summer in the Yakima, Columbia, and Walla Walla Valleys can be hot, with the thermometer climbing into the 90s and even the 100s, although nights are pleasantly cool. Summer thunderstorms are not infrequent in the Columbia and Walla Walla Valleys. Winter temperatures normally range from the low to mid-teens (and drop even lower during cold spells). The Columbia Valley, the lower Yakima Valley, and the Horse Heaven Hills sometimes experience dust storms that occur unexpectedly and can make driving hazardous.

Crossing the Cascade Mountain passes is easy during the summer but can be next to impossible in the winter, when they're often closed for avalanche control. Spring and fall may bring late and early snowstorms that slow traffic until the roads are cleared. Weather in the Cascades is cold and snowy in winter, generally cool in summer. Year-round, the weather may differ on western and eastern slopes; if it's cloudy west of a pass, the sun might be shining in the east.

You can visit Washington Wine Country during any time of the year, though driving isn't always easy from mid-November through mid-January. Because few visitors make the trip during this time, many wineries reduce their hours or close entirely, except for holiday open houses and other special events.

■ GETTING THERE AND AROUND

■ BY AIR
Seattle-Tacoma International Airport (SEA) is served by most of the major air carriers and their affiliates. *17801 Pacific Highway South; 206-431-4444 or 206-433-5388, www.seatac.org.*

Spokane Airport (GEG) is served by a few major airlines or their affiliates, and by smaller carriers. *9000 West Airport Drive; 509-455-6455, www.spokaneairports.net.*

Summers in the Yakima, Columbia, and Walla Walla Valleys can be hot, with temperatures sometimes climbing into the 90s and higher.

■ By Car

The main routes into Washington include I-90 from Idaho, I-5 from Oregon and Canada, and I-84 in Oregon (connecting to I-5, I-205, or I-82). The main north-south route through the state is I-5.

Route 542, the Mount Baker Highway, winds east from Bellingham through the Nooksack Valley and its vineyards. Route 20 runs west from I-5 at Burlington to the San Juan Island ferries in Anacortes and south to Whidbey Island. From Seattle, I-405, Route 520, and Route 522 lead to the Woodinville winery region.

You can reach the eastern Washington wine regions from Seattle via I-90 (across Snoqualmie Pass) and then I-82, which runs south and east from Ellensburg to Yakima, the Tri-Cities, and on to Oregon. You can also reach Yakima and beyond by taking U.S. 12 east from I-5, south of Chehalis, over White Pass. From Oregon, you can reach the Yakima Valley via U.S. 97, over Satus Pass, and both the lower Yakima Valley and the Columbia Valley via I-82 and U.S. 395. The Walla Walla Valley can be reached from the west (Pasco) and the east (Clarkston) on U.S. 12, and from Oregon (from I-84 at Pendleton) via Oregon's Route 11 to Washington's Route 125, or via U.S. 730 from I-82 at Umatilla.

■ By Train

Amtrak provides westbound service into Seattle from Chicago and northbound from Los Angeles. An additional train, running north-south between Eugene, Oregon, and Vancouver, British Columbia, makes many stops in Washington. *800-872-7245; www.amtrak.com.*

■ By Bus

Greyhound has the greatest number of scheduled bus routes in the state, including ones off I-82 and U.S. 12. *800-231-2222; www.greyhound.com.*

■ By Ferry

You can reach the wineries in the San Juan Islands by ferry from Anacortes, and the one on Bainbridge Island by road from the Kitsap Peninsula to the west or, more easily, by ferry from the downtown Seattle waterfront. *Schedules and rates: Washington State Ferries, 206-464-6400 or, in Washington, 800-843-3779. www. wsdot.wa.gov/ferries.*

■ RESTAURANTS

ENTRÉE PRICES PER PERSON		
$ = less than $15	**$$** = $15–$25	**$$$** = over $25

■ SEATTLE

Flying Fish. This noisy, popular Belltown fish house serves intriguing dishes that can be ordered in appetizer portions or as large platters to share with friends. *2234 First Avenue; 206-728-8595. Seafood.* **$$**

Ponti Seafood Grill. Seattle's brightest seafood house, overlooking a tree-lined section of the ship canal linking Lake Union to Puget Sound, serves Pacific Northwest seafood prepared with Asian and Mediterranean touches. The wine list is strong on Washington vintages. On a sunny day, you can sit outside and watch the boats go by. *3014 Third Avenue North; 206-284-3000. Seafood.* **$$**

Ray's Boathouse. Ray's has a reputation for serving the freshest seafood in town. It also has one of Seattle's best wine lists, and great views across Shilshole Bay—with luck, you can watch orcas swim by. *6049 Seaview Avenue NW; 206-789-3770. Seafood.* **$$**

Rover's. The dining room is small at Seattle's best French–Pacific Northwest restaurant, so reservations are essential. Excellent but pricey, Rover's has a superb, well-chosen wine list. *2808 East Madison Street; 206-325-7442. French–Pacific Northwest.* **$$$**

■ EASTSIDE

KIRKLAND
Cafe Juanita. The Eastside's favorite Italian dinner house has a winery (Cavatappi) in the basement. Meat, fowl, and fish are prepared with equal flair, and there's an excellent Italian and Northwest wine list. *9702 NE 120th Place; 425-823-1505. Northern Italian.* **$$**

Third Floor Fish Cafe. The food is so good that you might end up neglecting the sweeping views across Lake Washington. Seafood is the staple, but the chefs also do well by meat. *205 Lake Street South; 425-822-3553. Seafood.* **$$**

Yarrow Bay Grill and Beach Cafe. The grill is upstairs, with great views across Lake Washington; the café is downstairs, close to the water. Both are casual, fun places with delicious food. *1270 Carillon Point; 425-889-9052. Pacific Northwest Eclectic.* **$$**

WOODINVILLE

Armadillo Barbecue. Funky and down-to-earth, this neighborhood restaurant serves some of the best barbecue in the area. *13109 NE 175th Street; 425-481-1417. Barbecue.* **$**

Barking Frog. The Willow Lodge's comfortable, woodsy restaurant serves excellent food and has a well-selected Northwest wine list. *14582 NE 145th Street; 425-424-2999. Pacific Northwest.* **$$**

Herbfarm. The regionally famous restaurant serves elegantly prepared nine-course tasting dinners. *14590 NE 145th Street; 425-485-5300. Pacific Northwest.* **$$$**

■ PUGET SOUND AND THE SOUTHERN LOWLANDS

BELLINGHAM

Fino Wine Bar. The cozy dining room of the Chrysalis Hotel overlooks Bellingham Bay and is a great place to watch sea ducks, cormorants, and the weekly sailboat races while nibbling tapas and sipping wine. *8041 Tenth Street; 360-676-9463. Pacific Northwest–Mediterranean.* **$$**

BOW

Chuckanut Manor. The dining room at this converted early-20th-century blufftop home above Samish Bay is cozy, and the bar has birdfeeders outside its picture windows. Service is friendly, and the local seafood and grilled steaks are tasty. *302 Chuckanut Drive; 360-766-6191. Pacific Northwest.* **$$**

Oyster Bar. The food at this intimate restaurant south of Bellingham ranges from local seafood to hearty steaks. The service is refined, the wine list extensive, and the views across the water to the San Juan Islands are unparalleled, especially at sunset. *240 Chuckanut Drive, Bow; 360-766-6185. Pacific Northwest.* **$$**

FRIDAY HARBOR, SAN JUAN ISLAND

Duck Soup Inn. The imaginative menu here, which changes often, might include dishes such as griddle-fried fish cakes with house-cured salmon; grilled filet mignon

with horseradish-tarragon cream sauce; or wild boar, slow-cooked with ginger, star anise, and cinnamon. *3090 Roche Harbor Road; 360-378-4878. Pacific Northwest.* **$**

LANGLEY, WHIDBEY ISLAND

Cafe Langley. Small and comfortable, this streetfront restaurant serves everything from eggplant and hummus to local mussels, Dungeness crab, and salmon. *113 First Street; 360-221-3090. Pacific Northwest–Mediterranean.* **$–$$**

LOPEZ VILLAGE, LOPEZ ISLAND

Bay Cafe. Mussels, salmon, and other local seafood are served here, along with steaks grilled and sauced to perfection and a full array of vegetarian dishes. The menu changes weekly. The wine list is well thought out, and the prices for the food and wine are reasonable. *9 Old Post Road, Suite C; 360-468-3700. Eclectic.* **$**

SEAVIEW

42nd Street Cafe. This small, comfortable restaurant serves some of the best seafood in the region. Chef Cheri Walker runs the kitchen; her husband, Blaine, oversees the dining room and chooses Northwest wines. *4201 Pacific Way; 360-642-2323. Pacific Northwest–Seafood.* **$**

SHELTON

Xinh's Clam & Oyster House. This small restaurant does a great job with the Olympic Peninsula's seafood. With a little help from Asian seasonings, chef Xinh Dwelley has the perfect touch for bringing out its best flavors. *221 West Railroad Avenue; 360-427-8709. Seafood.* **$$**

■ COLUMBIA RIVER GORGE

STEVENSON

Dolce Skamania Lodge. The dining room at this golf resort has a fine view of the river and mountains. This is your best bet on the Washington side of the Columbia River Gorge. The cuisine isn't always inspired, but the portions are large. *1131 SW Skamania Lodge Way; 509-427-2547. Continental.* **$$**

VANCOUVER

Hudson's Bar and Grill. The elegant restaurant at the Heathman Lodge serves the area's best food, and the wine list includes some uncommon Northwest bottlings. *7805 Greenwood Drive; 360-816-6100. Pacific Northwest.* **$$**

■ YAKIMA VALLEY

GRANDVIEW

Dykstra House. The chef at this long-established restaurant in a remodeled 1914 home prepares delectable dishes made with local produce. The breads are baked on the premises. *114 Birch Avenue; 509-882-2082. American.* **$**

PROSSER

Blue Goose Restaurant. All-American prime rib, steaks, and seafood, along with some Italian dishes, are served at this family restaurant that has the lower Yakima Valley's largest local wine list. The desserts are decadent. *306 Seventh Street; 509-786-1774. American.* **$**

Vintner's Inn at Hinzerling Winery. The prix-fixe, six-course meals at this winery B&B are made from fresh local products, including organic fruits and vegetables from the on-site garden. Dinner is served on Friday and Saturday nights only; reservations are required. *1524 Sheridan Avenue; 509-786-2163. Pacific Northwest.* **$**

SUNNYSIDE

Snipes Mountain Brewery. Hearty steaks and burgers, along with sausage dishes, are served here. *2150 Yakima Valley Highway; 509-837-2739. American.* **$**

YAKIMA

Birchfield Manor. A remodeled farmhouse a few miles northeast of town holds this stylish restaurant that serves French-inspired dinners made from local ingredients. The wine list includes many hard-to-find Washington wines. *2018 Birchfield Road; 509-452-1960. Continental–Pacific Northwest.* **$$**

Gasperetti's. This streetfront restaurant has stayed at the top of the Yakima dining and social scene for several decades. *1013 North First Street; 509-248-0628. Italian–Pacific Northwest.* **$$**

ZILLAH

El Ranchito. A large cafeteria-style Mexican restaurant, tortilla factory, deli, and import shop at the east end of town, El Ranchito is a favorite hangout for locals, visitors, and seasonal farmworkers. The food is as good as it is inexpensive. *1319 East First Avenue; 509-829-5880. Mexican.* **$**

Squeeze Inn. The big draws at this unpretentious family-operated restaurant established in 1932 are prime rib and steaks, excellent soups and salads, and fresh seafood. The hearty breakfasts and lunches are popular. *611 East First Avenue; 509-829-6226. American.* **$**

■ RED MOUNTAIN

For restaurants near the Red Mountain wineries, see the Yakima Valley and Columbia Valley entries.

■ COLUMBIA VALLEY/TRI-CITIES

KENNEWICK

Blue Moon. Seven-course meals are served every Friday and Saturday night at this formal dining room that's been doing business here for years. *20 North Auburn; 509-582-6598. Continental.* **$$**

Casa Chapala. The fare is delicious at this friendly Mexican family restaurant where the tortillas are made fresh daily. *107 East Columbia Drive; 509-582-7848. Mexican.* **$**

Henry's. Steak, seafood, and pasta are served at this popular restaurant. *3013 West Clearwater Avenue; 509-735-1996. American.* **$$**

RICHLAND

Atomic Ale Brewpub & Eatery. Good microbrews and pub food—sandwiches, soups, steaks, wood-fired pizzas—are served in a congenial atmosphere. *1015 Lee Boulevard; 509-946-5465. American.* **$**

Rattlesnake Mountain Brewing Company. A popular local hangout, this brewpub with views of the Columbia River and Rattlesnake Mountain serves soups, sandwiches, burgers, and steaks. *2696 North Columbia Center Boulevard; 509-783-5747. American.* **$**

Samovar Russian Fine Dining & Bakery. Good Central and Eastern European food is served at this comfortable spot. *1340 Jadwin Avenue; 509-946-6655. Eastern European.* **$**

■ WALLA WALLA VALLEY

DAYTON

Patit Creek Restaurant. Chef and owner Bruce Hiebert has the perfect touch with beef, lamb, and chicken. His wife, Heather, makes the desserts, and her huckleberry and raspberry pies are regional legends. The restaurant, the best in the region, has an excellent list of local wines. *725 East Dayton Avenue; 509-382-2625. American.* **$$**

WALLA WALLA

Grapefields. This small wine bar in a handsome old building on Walla Walla's main drag has made a name for itself with its selection of tapas, antipasti, salads, and pizzas. *4 East Main Street; 509-522-3993. American-Mediterranean.* **$**

Merchants Ltd. Inexpensive breakfasts and lunches are served six days a week at this bakery and classic deli that becomes jammed on Saturday mornings. Merchants has a very good selection of local wines. *21 East Main Street; 509-525-0900. American.* **$**

Whitehouse-Crawford Restaurant. The chef here creates seasonal menus and has a fine touch with local white asparagus, morels, free-range chicken, and beef. The Walla Walla Valley wine list is extensive. *55 Cherry Street; 509-529-4193. Pacific Northwest.* **$$**

Pea and wheat fields in Walla Walla County.

■ LODGING

Hotels and motels throughout the state, both chains and independents, tend to be ordinary. They're fancier in the downtown areas of such cities as Seattle, Richland, and Walla Walla. In the Cascade Mountains and along the Columbia River, motels and hotels often have the feel of cozy lodges. Washington has many good B&Bs, most of them—especially in the Seattle area, the islands, and the Yakima and Walla Walla Valleys—catering to upscale travelers. Washington also has many country inns, a vaguely defined category. They're similar to B&Bs but usually have more rooms, or perhaps a restaurant and a bar.

With proper planning, you can rent cabins and houses in the Wine Country or in the mountains. First-rate lodging is still hard to find in eastern Washington, but the situation is changing, especially around Walla Walla.

> **PRICES DESIGNATIONS FOR LODGING, PER COUPLE**
> **$**= less than $100   **$$** = $100–$150   **$$$** = 150–$200   **$$$$** = over $200

■ SEATTLE

Inn at the Market. Many rooms at this boutique hotel look out over Elliott Bay, but the main attraction is the location—right in Pike Place Market. *86 Pine Street; 206-443-3600. 70 rooms.* **$$$$**

■ EASTSIDE

BELLEVUE
Bellevue Club Hotel. Utterly luxurious, this small hotel next to the Bellevue Athletic Club is *the* place to stay on the east side of Seattle. If you stay here, you can use the athletic club's exercise equipment—which may come in handy after food and wine tasting. *11200 SE Sixth Street; 425-454-4424 or 800-579-1110. 67 rooms.* **$$$$**

WOODINVILLE
Willows Lodge. This rustic lodge opened with much fanfare in 2001, but while the inn is popular with the software crowd visiting nearby Microsoft headquarters, travelers used to Napa and Sonoma lodgings have been less excited. Still, it's the only hotel within walking or biking distance of Woodinville wineries. *14580 NE 145th Street; 877-424-3930. 88 rooms.* **$$$$**

■ PUGET SOUND AND THE SOUTHERN LOWLANDS

BELLINGHAM

Chrysalis Inn & Spa. Overlooking Bellingham Bay from the atop a bluff, this modern Craftsman-style hotel has some of the best rooms in town. It also has Bellingham's best spa, at which you can avail yourself of a variety of massage and therapy services. *804 Tenth Street; 360-756-1005 or 888-808-0005. 43 rooms.* **$$$–$$$$**

Hotel Bellwether. This hotel, completed in 2001, sits right in the middle of Bellingham's Squalicum Harbor, so it's popular with boaters who tie up at the dock to spend the night in one of the very comfortable rooms—or just to enjoy a meal at the bistro. *1 Bellwether Way, off Roeder Avenue; 360-392-3100 or 877-411-1200. 68 rooms.* **$$–$$$**

FRIDAY HARBOR, SAN JUAN ISLAND

Friday Harbor House. Small and modern, this hotel on a bluff has rooms over-looking the harbor but is within walking distance of downtown Friday Harbor and the ferry landing. *130 West Street; 360-378-8455 or 866-722-7356. 20 rooms.* **$$$**

LANGLEY, WHIDBEY ISLAND

Inn at Langley. A rustic waterfront lodge with austere yet surprisingly comfortable rooms, the inn is within walking distance of downtown Langley and its shops and restaurants. *400 First Street; 360-221-3033. 24 rooms.* **$$$$**

■ COLUMBIA RIVER GORGE

STEVENSON

Dolce Skamania Lodge. High above the river, with splendid views of the Gorge and the mountains, the Skamania Lodge is known for its golf course, but the rooms are comfortable and there are several hiking trails on the grounds. *1131 SW Skamania Lodge Way; 509-427-2547 or 800-221-7117. 195 rooms.* **$$–$$$**

VANCOUVER

Heathman Lodge. Tucked off I-205 behind malls and business parks, this lodge is surprisingly quiet and rustic despite the suburban surroundings. It makes for a per-fect stopover before you tackle Gorge wineries—especially because the Heathman has a first-rate restaurant, Hudson's. *7801 NE Greenwood Drive; 360-254-3100 or 888-475-3100. 133 rooms.* **$–$$$**

■ **YAKIMA VALLEY**

SUNNYSIDE
Sunnyside Inn Bed & Breakfast. A doctor and his wife originally lived in this structure built in 1919 and now a very comfortable inn. *800 East Edison Avenue; 509-839-5557 or 800-221-4195. 8 rooms.* **$–$$**

YAKIMA
Birchfield Manor. The manor is known for its elegant restaurant in a remodeled farmhouse, but it also has guest rooms—five fine ones upstairs in the old house, and six more luxurious ones in a modern building next door. *2018 Birchfield Road; 509-452-1960. 11 rooms.* **$$–$$$**

■ **RED MOUNTAIN**
For lodgings convenient to Red Mountain wineries, see the Yakima Valley and Columbia Valley entries.

■ **COLUMBIA VALLEY/TRI-CITIES**

RICHLAND
Hampton Inn. Right on the Columbia River, this hotel is south of downtown Richland at the southern end of Howard Amon Park and the riverfront path. Some of the rooms have spectacular river views. *486 Bradley Boulevard; 509-943-4400 or 800-426-7866. 130 rooms.* **$–$$**

Red Lion Hotel Richland Hanford House. Some rooms at this downtown hotel on the Columbia River's west bank have water views. *802 George Washington Way; 509-946-7611 or 800-733-5466. 150 rooms.* **$$**

Shilo Inn Rivershore. Tucked below a Columbia River levee south of downtown, this motel is close to I-82 yet surprisingly secluded and quiet. *50 Comstock Street; 509-946-4661 or 800-222-2244. 150 rooms.* **$**

■ **WALLA WALLA VALLEY**

WALLA WALLA
Marcus Whitman Hotel. After a recent restoration, this 1928 hotel is once again the crown jewel of downtown Walla Walla. *6 West Rose Street; 509-525-2200 or 866-826-9422. 91 rooms.* **$–$$$**

■ RESERVATION SERVICES

Karen Brown's Guides. *www.karenbrown.com/pnw.*
A Pacific Reservation Service. *206-439-7677 or 800-684-2932;*
www.seattlebedandbreakfast.com.
Unique Northwest Inns. *877-286-4783; www.uniqueinns.com.*

■ HOTEL AND MOTEL CHAINS

Best Western. *800-528-1234; www.bestwestern.com.*
Comfort Inn. *800-228-5150; www.comfortinn.com.*
Days Inn. *800-325-2525; www.daysinn.com.*
Doubletree. *800-222-8733; www.doubletree.com.*
Econolodge. *800-446-6900; www.econolodge.com.*
Embassy Suites. *800-362-2779; www.embassysuites.com.*
Hampton Inn. *800-426-7866; www.hamptoninn.com.*
Hilton. *800-445-8667; www.hilton.com.*
Holiday Inn. *800-465-4329; www.6c.com.*
La Quinta. *800-531-5900; www.lq.com.*
Marriott. *800-228-9290; www.marriott.com.*
Quality Inns. *800-228-5151; www.qualityinn.com.*
Radisson. *800-333-3333; www.radisson.com.*
Ramada Inns. *800-272-6232; www.ramada.com.*
Sheraton. *800-325-3535; www.sheraton.com.*
Shilo Inns. *800-222-2244; www.shiloinns.com.*
Travelodge. *800-255-3050; www.travelodge.com.*
WestCoast. *800-325-4000; www.westcoasthotels.com.*
Westin. *800-228-3000; www.westin.com.*

■ OFFICIAL TOURISM INFORMATION

Washington State Tourism. *360-725-5052 or 800-544-1800; www.tourism.wa.gov.*
Bellingham/Whatcom County. *360-671-3990 or 800-487-2032;*
www.bellingham.org.
Grandview. *509-882-2100; www.grandview.wa.us.*
Greater Pasco Area. *509-547-9755; www.pascochamber.org.*
Kitsap Peninsula. *360-297-8200 or 800-416-5615; www.visitkitsap.com.*

Prosser. *509-786-3177; www.prosserchamber.org.*
San Juan Islands. *360-468-3663 or 888-468-3701; www.guidetosanjuans.com.*
Seattle. *206-461-5840; www.seeseattle.org.*
Sunnyside. *800-457-8089; www.sunnysidechamber.com.*
Tri-Cities. *509-735-8486 or 800-254-5824; www.visittri-cities.com.*
Walla Walla. *877-998-4748; www.wallawalla.org.*
Woodinville Chamber of Commerce. *425-481-8300; woodinvillechamber.org*
Yakima Valley. *800-221-0751; www.visityakima.com.*

■ WINE ASSOCIATIONS

Columbia Gorge Winegrowers Association. *503-685-7803.*
Columbia Valley Winery Association. *509-628-8082; www.columbiavalleywine.com.*
Klickitat Wine Alliance. *509-773-1976; 877-627-9445; www.gorgewine.com.*
Puget Sound Wine Growers Association. *360-468-3644; www.pswg.org.*
Walla Walla Valley Wine Alliance. *509-526-3117; www.wallawallawine.com.*
Washington Association of Wine Grape Growers. *509-782-8234; www.wawgg.org.*
Washington Wine Archives. *www.wawinearchives.com.*
Washington Wine Commission. *206-667-9463; www.washingtonwine.org.*
Yakima Valley Wine Association. *800-258-7270; www.yakimavalleywine.com.*

■ USEFUL WEB SITES

Pike Place Market. Fun, informative site about Seattle's famous marketplace. *www.pikeplacemarket.org.*

Seattle Post-Intelligencer. Major daily newspaper. *www.seattlepi.com.*

Washington State Department of Transportation. Road conditions and highway cams, plus ferry schedules, information on bicycle touring, and more. *360-705-7000; www.wsdot.wa.gov.*

Washington State Parks. Information about state parks and campgrounds as well as cabins, yurts, and houses for rent in them; bulletins about which parks have been temporarily or seasonally closed due to budgetary cutbacks. *360-902-8844; www.parks.wa.gov.*

■ SHIPPING WINE

Sending wine home from the wineries you visit is becoming easier as more states are liberalizing the rules for shipping wine interstate as a result of legislative actions and court decisions. In 2003, several states opened their borders to shipments of wine direct to the consumer from other states. Texas also allowed shipments, though only to "wet" counties. Currently, many states, including California, Oregon, and Washington, allow residents to accept at least some out-of-state wine deliveries.

Laws regarding the purchase of wines online have also begun to liberalize. In 2003, many states began allowing shipments, and, depending on the outcome of several court cases, including ones in Florida, Michigan, and New York, online wine shipping could expand. Because laws about interstate shipping of wine vary so greatly from state to state—and because the penalties for noncompliance in some states can be severe—if you're going to ship wine home, it is wise to do so either through the winery or a professional shipper.

Budding grapes at Kiona Vineyards

■ FESTIVALS AND EVENTS

■ MARCH
Capital Food & Wine Festival, Lacey. This popular event with regional wines and local foods takes place at St. Martin's College. *360-438-4366 or 800-220-7722; www.stmartin.edu/alumni/food_wine.htm.*

■ APRIL
Klickitat Wine Alliance Spring Barrel Tasting, Columbia River Gorge. A down-home affair at a number of small wineries, with tastings in their barrel rooms. *509-773-1976 or 877-627-9445; www.gorgewine.com.*

Taste Washington, Seattle. A large-scale event organized by the Washington Wine Commission, with fresh seafood, an oyster bar, cheese and caviar tastings, and wine and food pairings; some 150 wineries and restaurants participate. *206-667-9463; www.washingtonwine.org.*

Washington State Apple Blossom Festival, Wenatchee. The oldest such festival in the United States, with a grand parade, an apple blossom queen, and apple pie. *509-662-3616; www.appleblossom.org.*

Yakima Valley Spring Barrel Tasting, Yakima County. Regardless of iffy late-April weather, a popular event, at which wineries offer samples of yet-to-be-bottled vintages. *800-258-7270; www.yakimavalleywine.com/springbarrel.html.*

■ MAY
Walla Walla Balloon Stampede. A sell-out event that's been held for more than three decades, the stampede attracts as many as 40,000 people. One draw is the night glow of a dozen balloons lit from within, accompanied by fireworks; the champagne reception at the Marcus Whitman Hotel and Conference Center is another. *509-525-0850 or 877-998-4748; www.wwchamber.com/wwbs.htm.*

Walla Walla Spring Release Weekend, Walla Walla Valley. The one weekend when most valley wineries—even the most exclusive ones—are open to the public, pouring samples of just-released (or about-to-be-released) wines. *509-526-3117; www.wallawallawine.com.*

■ JUNE

ArtWalla, Walla Walla. "Nonstop art for 10 days," along with a culinary celebration. Highlights include an event at which restaurants set up booths and serve signature dishes; a wine reception and dinner; juried and community art shows; and a downtown concert. *509-525-0850 or 877-998-4748; www.artwalla.com.*

Sunshine & Wine, Yakima. A food-and-wine event held in conjunction with the Annual Washington Wine Competition, whose winners are announced during the festival. *509-248-7160; www.sunshineandwine.com.*

■ JULY

Red, Wine, and Blues, Stevenson. An annual wine, food, and music festival held at the Columbia River Gorge Interpretive Center, overlooking the Columbia River. *800-991-2338; www.columbiagorge.org.*

■ AUGUST

Auction of Washington Wines, Woodinville. An annual gala, held at Chateau Ste. Michelle, featuring two events: an informal picnic and a black-tie dinner and auction. Both sell out well in advance. *206-667-9463, ext. 204.*

Northwest Wine Festival, Seattle. The granddaddy of all Northwest wine events, with judgings and tastings, presented by the granddaddy of all Northwest wine organizations, the Enological Society. *425-603-9558; www.enosoc.org.*

Prosser Wine and Food Fair. This fun down-home event is so popular it's held in the local high-school stadium to accommodate the large crowds. *800-408-1517; www.prosserchamber.org/wine-food_fair.htm.*

■ SEPTEMBER

Catch the Crush, Tri-Cities/Columbia Valley. One of the state's most enjoyable harvest festivals showcases local foods and wines. *509-628-8082 or 866-360-6611; www.columbiavalleywine.com.*

Harvest Wine Tour, Columbia Gorge. Several wineries of the Klickitat Wine Alliance open their cellars and pour some uncommon bottlings. *509-773-1976 or 877-627-9445; www.gorgewine.com.*

Huckleberry Festival, Bingen. Berries, freshly picked on the slopes of Mount Adams, local wines, local foods, and local spirit at a very folksy celebration. *509-493-3630.*

■ **October**
Annual PONCHO Wine Auction for the Arts, Seattle. A social gala and auction of wines, to benefit local arts. *206-623-6233; www.poncho.org.*

■ **November**
Thanksgiving in Wine Country, Yakima Valley. An autumn event at which you might get to taste some of the just fermented wines of the new vintage. *800-258-7270; www.yakimavalleywine.com.*

Thanksgiving Open House, Columbia Gorge. Local wineries offer a taste of some of their rarer wines. *509-773-1976 or 877-627-9445; www.gorgewine.com.*

Tri-Cities Wine Festival. This is one of the Northwest's premier wine events, with tastings, food and wine pairings, and judging of regional wines. *800-254-5824; www.visittri-cities.com.*

■ **December**
Holiday Barrel Tasting, Walla Walla Valley. For those curious about how the current vintage is faring, a chance to visit the wineries on the first weekend in December and taste for themselves—as well as to sample older, maturing vintages. *509-526-3117; www.wallawallawine.com.*

G L O S S A R Y

Acidity. The tartness of a wine, derived from the fruit acids of the grape. Acids stabilize a wine (i.e., keep it from going flat), serving as a counterpoint to its sugars, if there are any, and bringing out its flavors. Acid is to wine what salt is to cooking—a proper amount is necessary, but too much spoils the taste. Tartaric acid is the major acid in wine, but malic, lactic, and citric acids also occur, in greatly variable concentrations.

Aftertaste. The way a wine lingers on the palate after you have swirled it around in your mouth. Good wines have a long-lasting aftertaste of many complex flavors and aromas.

Aging. The process by which wines react to oxygen at a very slow rate. If properly stored, some wines improve with aging, becoming smoother and more complex and developing a pleasing bouquet. But most wines do not age well. Even a small amount of oxidation can spoil lighter wines, which are much more enjoyable when young and fresh. When aged for just a short time, they may lose their fruit and thus their appeal. Their color dulls: whites turn brownish, rosés orange, reds brown. Today even some of the wines once made in a heavier style—e.g., cabernet sauvignon—are sometimes made to be drunk after 5 to 10 rather than 20 to 50 years. Wine is most commonly aged in oak vats or in old or new oak barrels, slowly interacting with the air through the pores in the wood. New oak contains tannins and flavoring elements that the wine leaches from the wood. Too much exposure to these oak extracts can overpower the varietal character of a wine. Old oak retains fewer foreign flavors.

Alcohol. Ethyl alcohol is a colorless, volatile, pungent spirit that gives wine its stimulating effect and some of its flavor, and acts as a preservative, stabilizing the wine and allowing it to age. Alcohol content must be stated on the label, expressed as a percentage of volume, except when a wine is designated table wine (*see* Table Wine).

American Viticultural Area (AVA). An AVA is a region with unique soil, climate, and other grape-growing conditions designated as such by the Alcohol and Tobacco Tax and Trade Bureau. The term is basically synonymous with "appellation," though

appellation sometimes refers colloquially to a wine region that has no legal geographical standing. When a label lists an appellation—e.g., the Yakima Valley—85 percent of the grapes the wine is made from must come from that region.

Appellation. *See* American Viticultural Area.

Argol. A crude form of tartar, often deposited on the sides of wine barrels during aging.

Aroma. The scent of young wine derived directly from the fresh fruit. It diminishes with fermentation and is replaced by a more complex bouquet as the wine ages. The term may also be used to describe special fruity odors in a wine, like black cherry, green olive, ripe raspberry, or apple.

Assemblage. *See* Blending.

Astringent. What a layman might call "sour," though experts use the term "sour" only for a spoiled wine.

AVA. *See* American Viticultural Area.

Balance. The harmony of elements in a wine. A well-balanced wine has a special mouth feel, a simultaneous appeal to the olfactory, gustatory, and tactile senses.

Barbera. An Italian wine grape from the Piedmont. Recent plantings at the eastern end of the Columbia River Gorge have shown that it grows well in that region's warm climate, which is protected from late spring and early fall frosts by the mitigating influence of the river. Early bottlings indicate that it can give deeply colored, full-bodied wines with tarry, spicy, earthy character, a good acid backbone, and a pronounced varietal character.

Barrel. A cylindrical storage container with bulging sides; usually made from American, French, Slavonic, or Baltic oak. A full barrel holds the equivalent of 240 regular 750 ml bottles.

Barrel Fermenting. The fermenting of wine in small oak barrels instead of large tanks or vats, allowing the winemaker to keep grape lots separate before blending them. This method, traditionally used by small European wineries, has recently become a fad among West Coast winemakers. The trend may or may not survive the spiraling cost of oak barrels.

Big. The quality of having considerable body, forward aromas, and high alcohol content. Big wines are not necessarily good wines, because the excess can make the flavors coarse.

Binning. Cellaring bottles of wine at the winery for aging. The bottles should be laid on their sides to keep the corks moist, since dried-out corks may allow air to leak in, spoiling the wine. Storage temperature and humidity should be kept as even as possible.

Blending. The careful mixing of several wines to create a wine of greater complexity or a more enjoyable one, as when a heavy wine is blended with a lighter one to create a more readily approachable medium-bodied wine. Not all wines containing more than one grape variety are blends. In the vineyards of Bordeaux and in some Washington vineyards, different varieties of grapes are interplanted and crushed together; this mixing is not considered a blending, since it occurs before the wine is fermented. The blending of sparkling wines is called *assemblage.*

Blush Wines. Pink wine, usually sweet and with little character, made from prime red-wine grapes that cannot find a market as red wine. Many so-called white zinfandels are actually blush wines. Better pink wines are usually labeled rosés.

Body. The substance of a wine as experienced by the palate. A full body is an advantage in the case of some reds, a disadvantage in many lighter whites.

Bottle Sizes. Metric sizes have replaced the traditional bottle sizes of gallon, quart, fifth, et al., though the old names linger:

Tenth . . . . .375 ml. of wine	

Fifth . . . . .750 ml. (25.4 oz.)
The most commonly used wine bottle

Magnum . . . .1.50 liters (50.72 oz.)

Half Gallon . . .1.75 liters (59.2 oz.)

Double Magnum . . . . .3.0 liters
also called Jeroboam

Rehoboam . . . . .4.5 liters (approx.)
The equivalent of five 750 ml. bottles

Other, larger-sized bottles include the approximately 9-liter Salmanzar and the Nebuchadnezzar, which holds from 13 to 15 liters of wine, depending on where, when, and by whom it was made.

Bouquet. The different odors a mature wine gives off when opened. They should be diverse but pleasing, complex but not confused, and should give an indication of the wine's grape variety, origin, age, and quality.

Brix. A method of telling whether grapes are ready for picking by measuring their sugars. Multiplying the Brix number by .55 yields the potential alcohol content of the wine (though the finished wine may be slightly higher or lower).

Brut. A dry sparkling wine. *See also* Demi-sec, Sec.

Butt. A large wine barrel or cask with a capacity of 100 to 140 gallons; the most common holds 500 liters (132 U.S. gallons).

Cabernet Franc. A noble grape of France's Bordeaux region that produces aromatic red wines that are softer and more subtle than those of the closely related cabernet sauvignon and age more quickly. Cabernet franc is often blended into cabernet sauvignon to soften the wine of that somewhat harsher grape. In Washington's Walla Walla and Yakima Valleys and in the Columbia Gorge, it produces an excellent, well-balanced wine.

Cabernet Sauvignon. The noble red-wine grape that has made the clarets of Bordeaux renowned. It grows very well in Washington's Columbia Valley and gives great wine in the Walla Walla and Yakima Valleys. Its wine is deeply red and tannic and requires a long period of aging to become fully enjoyable. For this reason it is often blended with cabernet franc, merlot, and other related red varieties, to soften it and to make it drinkable earlier. Cabernet sauvignon from a great year can age for a hundred years or longer.

Case. A carton of 12 bottles of wine. A magnum case contains six 1.5-liter magnum bottles.

Cask. A wine container, commonly made from oak staves.

Champagne. *See* Sparkling Wines.

Chardonnay. The noble French grape variety of the great white burgundies of Montrachet, Meursault, and Chablis, as well as the lesser whites of Pouilly-Fuissé and Mâcon. It is also one of the principal varieties of the Champagne region. Chardonnay is widely planted in eastern Washington, where it gives wine that can range from light and pleasing to big and extremely complex. Experimental plantings seem to indicate that this warm-climate grape might also do well in the warmer vineyards of the Puget Sound region.

Chenin Blanc. A noble old French white-grape variety that has recently fallen from grace in Washington because it does not make big wine, as chardonnay does. But in Washington it makes excellent fruity white wine that in good years may be aged and can develop a beautiful, complex bouquet.

Chilling. A common practice for sparkling wines and some whites, decried for reds by traditionalists, but indulged in by some very famous winemakers on hot summer days. (So if you'd like an ice cube in your wine—put it in!)

Claret. A name once applied by British connoisseurs to red wines from Bordeaux. The term came into disrepute after it was applied to bulk wines. It is, however, regaining respect as premium wineries bestow the name on their red blends.

Clarity. The lack of particles—both large and minute—floating in a wine; a requirement for a good wine. Wine should always be clear (though it can be dark or dense); it should never be cloudy.

Cloudiness. The presence of particles—often minute—that do not settle out of a wine, causing it to taste dusty or even muddy. To correct it, set the bottle, at a slant, in a place where it will not be disturbed, then let the sediments settle. This could take from a few minutes to several hours depending on the wine.

Decant the clear liquid on top and discard the sediments. If the wine remains cloudy, get rid of it—it has been badly made or is spoiled.

Columbia Valley AVA. A vast octopus of an appellation—the Pacific Northwest's largest. It stretches from Roosevelt Lake in the northeast to the mouth of the Okanogan River in the northwest, then south along the eastern Cascade foothills to the Yakima Valley and across the Columbia River into northern Oregon; from there, east to the Walla Walla Valley, and north up the Snake River almost to Idaho. It encompasses three independent AVAs, the Walla Walla Valley, the Yakima Valley, and Red Mountain. Its great variety of soils range from almost pure rock to deep alluvial silts and sands, its climates from very hot to quite cool. The kaleidoscopic variety of growing conditions allows a great number of different grape varieties to succeed in this viticultural region.

Complexity. Layers of different flavors and aromas in harmony with the overall balance of a wine, and perhaps, in an aged wine, a pleasing bouquet and a lingering aftertaste.

Controlled Fermentation. The fermentation of white wines at low temperatures, in chilled tanks, to

preserve the fruit and delicacy of the grape flavors and aromas. Reds may undergo uncontrolled fermentation, which results in high temperatures that help extract tannins and pigments from the grape skins, but this is undesirable for whites.

Cooperage. A collective term used to describe all the containers of a winery in which wine is stored and aged before bottling. It includes barrels, casks, vats, and tanks of different materials and sizes.

Corky or Corked. Affected by off flavors and aromas created by a leaky cork or cork infection. The contact between the wine and the air that such leakage allows will, with time, spoil the wine.

Crush. A colloquial West Coast winemaker's term denoting the vintage in which grapes are made into wine. Not all the grapes grown in the state go into wine. Some go to market fresh, others are made into raisins; these are not part of the crush but are counted as part of the grape harvest.

Cuvée. A sparkling wine that is a blend of different wines and sometimes different vintages. Most sparkling wines are cuvées, although in very good years some are vintage dated.

Decant. To slowly and carefully pour an aged wine from its bottle into a decanter. Decanting need be done only with old wines that have a sediment, which, when stirred up by careless handling, might cloud the wine. Careful decanting leaves the sediment in the bottle.

Demi-sec. Although sec means "dry," in the convoluted language of sparkling wine, demi-sec is sweet. More specifically, wine that contains 3.5 to 5 percent sugar.

Dessert Wines. Sweet wines that are big in flavor and aroma but may be quite low in alcohol, or wines that have been fortified *(see* Fortification) with brandy or neutral spirits and may be quite high (17–21 percent) in alcohol.

Dosage. A mixture of wine and sugar added to fermented wine in order to create bubbles, inducing a secondary fermentation in the bottle. *See* Sparkling Wines.

Dry. The term used to describe a wine that is not sweet, although it may contain some residual sugar. The American wine industry's long fight to wean consumers away from sweet wines has turned "dry" into an important enological concept.

Estate Bottled. A label term indicating that both the winery and the vineyards from which the grapes were harvested are in the same appellation (which must be printed on the label), that the winery owns or controls the vineyards, and that all the winemaking processes, from crushing to bottling, were done at a single winery facility.

Fermentation. The process—in which enzymes generated by yeast cells convert the grape sugars of must into alcohol and carbon dioxide—by which grape juice becomes wine. *See also* Controlled Fermentation.

Fermenter. Any vessel, small or large (such as a barrel, tank, or vat), in which wine is fermented.

Filtering, Filtration. A purification process in which wine is pumped through filters to rid it of suspended particles. If mishandled, filtration can remove a wine's flavor.

Fining. A traditional method of clarifying wine by adding crushed eggshells, isinglass, or other natural substances to a barrel. As these solids settle to the bottom, they take suspended particles with them, thus clarifying the wine. A slower, more tedious process than filtering, but one that makes better wine.

Flat. Said of a wine that lacks acid and is thus dull; also of a sparkling wine that has lost its bubbles.

Fortification. A process by which brandy or natural spirits are added to a wine to stop fermentation and increase its level of alcohol, making it more stable—less subject to spoilage and to separation of the solids from the liquids—than a regular table wine after a bottle has been opened. Before the modern American wine revolution, most Northwest wines were fortified.

Foxiness. The odd flavor of native American grapes or their hybrids, including Catawba, Concord, and Island Belle (Campbell Early). Wines made from these grapes are an acquired taste.

Free Run. Juice that runs from the crushed grapes before pressing. It is more intense in flavor than pressed juice and has fewer (or no) off flavors.

Fruity. Having aromatic nuances of fresh fruit—fig, raspberry, apple, et cetera. Fruitiness, a sign of quality in young wines, is replaced by bouquet in aged wines.

Fumé Blanc. Term coined by the Napa Valley's Robert Mondavi to describe a dry, crisp sauvignon blanc. It is now

used so indiscriminately, though, that it has lost any special meaning. In Washington it is commonly applied to sauvignon blanc that has been fermented and aged in oak.

Generic. A name or trade name for a wine that does not commonly reflect the grapes the wine is made from, the origin of the grapes, or its quality. In Washington it is usually labeled with a proprietary name.

Gewürztraminer. A German-Alsatian pinkish grape variety that makes excellent aromatic, almost spicy white wine in the Columbia Gorge and the Yakima Valley and shows promise in the cool Puget Sound growing region and elsewhere in Washington.

Green. Said of a wine made from unripe grapes, with a pronounced leafy flavor and a raw edge.

Grenache. A southern French red-wine grape of Spanish origin *(garnacha),* with limited plantings in the western Columbia Valley, where it makes appealing, very fruity wines.

Horizontal Tasting. A tasting of wines of the same vintage from several wineries.

Johannisberg Riesling. *See* Riesling.

Late Harvest, Select Late Harvest, Special Select Late Harvest. Wine made from grapes harvested later in the fall than the main lot, and thus higher in sugar levels. These terms are vague, however, and have no legal meaning in Washington; at worst, their usage on a wine label may simply indicate that the grapes grew too ripe and that the resulting wine is sweet and cloying.

Lees. The spent yeast and any grape solids that have dropped out of suspension while a wine has been aging in an oak barrel or a tank. White wines that are left on the lees for a time often improve in complexity; this method has become a popular way of aging chardonnay and sauvignon blanc.

Lemberger. Also called "Limburger," this German-Austrian red-wine grape makes rather indifferent wine in its home countries but pleasing wine in eastern Washington. The best Washington lemberger grapes come from the Celilo Vineyard in the Columbia Gorge.

Maderized. A term applied to a white or rosé wine that is past its prime and has become oxidized with an undesirable flavor and aroma of Madeira.

Malbec. A red Bordeaux grape commonly used in blending. On its own malbec makes deeply colored, somewhat tannic wine. Less aromatic than cabernet sauvignon, it is softer and ages earlier and is therefore commonly blended with cabernet in Bordeaux reds as well as in Washington meritage wines. In Washington's Columbia Valley it also makes very good wines on its own.

Malolactic Fermentation. A secondary fermentation in the tank or barrel that changes harsh malic acid into softer lactic acid and carbon dioxide, making the wine smoother. Because it lowers the perceptible level of a wine's acids, malolactic fermentation is frowned upon in regions where wines, especially whites, tend to have low acid to begin with. In cool regions, where wines have a high natural acidity, it is a boon to the winemaker, because it rounds out the wine, making it less acid and more complex at the same time.

Marsanne. A white-wine grape of France's northern Rhône Valley that can produce a full-bodied, overly heavy wine unless handled with care. It makes very good wine in eastern Washington.

Meritage. A high-quality red or white blend in which none of the wines included reach the 75-percent level required by federal law to label the bottle with the name of the grape variety. The meritage designation allows winemakers more flexibility than traditional varietal blends, but these wines are in no way inferior to varietal bottlings, and they often carry a vintage date.

Merlot. Known in its native France as *merlot noir,* for the dark, blue-black color of its berries, this grape is more productive than cabernet and yields a softer, more supple wine that may be drunk at a younger age. Until recent years, merlot was not widely planted in Washington, but it has now experienced such a boom that it may well replace chardonnay as America's favorite dinner wine. Walla Walla Valley merlot has a vociferous cult following.

Méthode Champenoise. *See* Sparkling Wines.

Microclimates. Highly localized climate conditions that affect the ripening of grapes—for example, conditions on a sunny, frost-free slope in a chilly, foggy valley; on a wind-sheltered nook near the sea; et cetera.

Washington State is known for its many microclimates.

Müller-Thurgau. A German vinifera hybrid widely planted in Puget Sound vineyards. It makes a pleasant white wine with a muscat-like flavor, which can resemble Rieslings grown in cool coastal climes.

Muscat Blanc. Also called **Muscat de Frontignan** or **Muscat Canelli**, this is an ancient, very aromatic grape that may have been brought to France by Greek colonists who settled Provence before the Roman empire. It has been planted in eastern Washington since at least the end of Prohibition, but never on a large scale. Perhaps its flavor is too pronounced for the American palate. In Washington it is distinguished by good acids, so even when it is picked overripe it makes a lusciously rich dessert wine with an intense bouquet.

Must. Crushed grapes and/or their juice, either ready to be or in the process of being fermented into wine.

Nebbiolo. The great red-wine grape of Italy's Piedmont region, where it makes such renowned wines as barolo, barbaresco, and gattinara. It has been planted for several decades in the Yakima Valley and more recently in the Columbia Valley, producing full-bodied, sturdy wines that are fairly high in alcohol and age splendidly. Look for wines from this grape grown in the Yakima Valley's Red Willow Vineyard and in the Horse Heaven Hills.

Noble. A term that, applied to grapes and wines, denotes both inherited status and quality. A noble grape variety produces good (in the right hands, great) wine almost everywhere it is planted. A noble wine—either varietal or blended—is one whose combination of flavors, aromas, mouth feel, and finish even a novice can identify as special.

Noble Rot. *Botrytis cinerea,* a beneficial fungus mold that attacks certain ripe grapes, perforating their skin. This shrivels the grapes through dehydration and concentrates the sugars and flavor elements in the remaining juice while preserving the grape's acids. This helps keep the resulting sweet wine from becoming cloying. (If the fungus strikes before the grapes are fully ripe, however, it can spoil them.)

Non-Vintage. Having no vintage date on the label, usually indicating that the wine is a blend from different vineyards, growing regions, or even vintages. This is not necessarily evidence of poor quality; it may represent an attempt to make wine of a consistent, recognizable quality year after year.

Nose. The overall fragrance (aroma or bouquet) given off by a wine, which is the better part of its flavor.

Oak. The most popular wood for making wine barrels, because, if used properly, it can impart desirable flavors to the wine stored in it and add to its complexity. If abused, it can make a wine taste woody and oaky.

Oaky. Said of a wine that has been aged in new oak for too long and tastes more of the vanilla-like flavors of the wood than of the grape. Once praised as a virtue in California chardonnays; now considered a fault.

Oxidized. Condition of a wine that had too much contact with the air, either as juice or through faulty winemaking or a leaky barrel or cork. Most often occurs with white wine, although it does happen to reds too. An oxidized wine has lost its freshness and is on its way to becoming maderized. Depending on how far the oxidation has progressed, such a wine should be either drunk immediately (preferably with strongly seasoned food) or discarded.

Pétillant. A French term indicating, like the German *spritzig,* a wine that is slightly sparkling. This quality can be refreshing in light silvaner, chenin blanc, or other chilled white carafe wine.

Petite Sirah. A noble red-wine grape of California whose origin is shrouded in mystery. It was once thought to be the true *syrah* grape of France, but it is not. Because it is a true vinifera grape, it may be a hybrid that occurred in a mid-19th-century California vineyard—much like the equally mysterious zinfandel. It has recently been planted in eastern Washington, where it makes excellent red wine.

pH. An indicator of a wine's acidity. It is a reverse measure—that is, the lower the pH level, the higher the acidity.

Phylloxera. A disease caused by the root louse *Phylloxera vastatrix,* native to the central and eastern United States. It attacks grapevine roots, first weakening, and ultimately destroying them. It was transported to France when the French experimented with native American grape varieties such as Concord and muscadine.

Pinot Noir. An ancient noble French grape variety that, under perfect conditions, makes some of the best red wine in the world. Though not widely planted in Washington (unlike Oregon), it can make excellent wines here. The best pinot noir vineyards are near La Center, north of Vancouver, Washington.

Pomace. The spent skins and grape solids from which the juice has been pressed, commonly returned to the fields as fertilizer.

Port. A richly sweet red or tawny Portuguese dessert wine, whose name is also applied—incorrectly—to various red Washington dessert wines.

Puget Sound AVA. A mostly maritime appellation that stretches from the Canadian border south to Thurston County and west to the Elwha River on the Olympic Peninsula, and includes the islands of Puget Sound and the Salish Sea. It is a generally cool growing region, though it includes some surprisingly warm vineyards. Wines produced here from local grapes are refreshing and fruity.

Racking. Moving wine from one tank or barrel to another, to leave deposits behind; the wine may or may not be fined or filtered in the process.

Red Mountain AVA. An appellation encompassing Red Mountain, a low ridge above the Yakima River, east of Prosser and west of the Tri-Cities, whose rocky, well-drained soils support excellent red-wine grapes. The mountain has several wineries, and its grapes are also eagerly sought by other wineries on both sides of the Cascade Mountains.

Residual Sugar. Sugar left over from fermentation that is above the 0.5 percent threshold of perception. In the 1990s, leaving it in became a popular way of finishing white and red table wines, because consumers, while claiming to like dry wines, actually prefer slightly sweet ones.

Riesling. Also called Johannisberg Riesling or White Riesling, the noble white-wine grape of Germany was introduced to Washington in the mid-19th century by immigrant vintners; but it was not until the 1970s that Washington vintners learned how to handle this cool-climate grape properly. Even though Riesling now gives great wine here, it has been upstaged by chardonnay, viognier, and other white-wine varieties more suited to eastern Washington's warm climes. When ripe Riesling grapes are affected by the noble rot, their juice becomes very concentrated, making for luscious, complex, richly sweet wine.

Rosé. French term for pink wine, usually made from black (red-wine) grapes whose juice has been left on the skins only long enough to give it a tinge of color. Rosés can be pleasant and versatile food wines, especially when they are made from premium grapes like cabernet sauvignon,

grenache, or pinot noir. In Washington, they are frequently made from cabernet franc.

Rounded. Said of a well-balanced, complete wine—a good wine, though not necessarily a distinctive or great one.

Roussanne. A noble white-wine grape of France's Rhône Valley that gives a full-bodied, distinguished wine. It makes pleasantly fruity and complex wine in eastern Washington.

Sangiovese. The principal red grape of Italy's Chianti district and of much of central Italy. Depending on how it is grown and vinified, this versatile grape can be made into vibrant, light- to medium-bodied wines as well as into long-lived, very complex reds (like Italy's renowned Brunello di Montalcino). Bottlings from the Yakima Valley's Red Willow vineyard and from the Walla Walla Valley have all the attributes of top-quality clarets.

Sauvignon Blanc. A noble white-wine grape of France's Bordeaux region. It most likely thrived on the banks of the Gironde estuary long before the Romans introduced viticulture to southwestern France. Sauvignon blanc does very well in eastern Washington, where it makes great food wines. A dry, sometimes austere wine made from this grape, usually fermented and aged in oak, is sometimes marketed as fumé blanc.

Sec. Although *sec* means "dry" in French, in speaking about wines sec indicates one that has from 1.7 to 3.5 percent sugar. In the language of sparkling wine, drier than demi-sec but not as dry as brut.

Sediment. Deposits that most red wines throw as they age in the bottle, thus clarifying their appearance, flavors, and aromas. Not a defect in an old wine or in a new wine that has been bottled unfiltered.

Sémillon. A white Bordeaux grape variety that, blended with sauvignon blanc, has made some of the best sweet wines in the world. Like Riesling, it can be affected by the noble rot, which concentrates its juices and intensifies its flavors and aromas. Sémillon also makes excellent dry seafood-friendly wines in Washington, both undiluted and blended with sauvignon blanc.

Siegerrebe. A German gewürztraminer hybrid that ripens well in cool climates. When well-made, this is a beautifully refreshing wine. Recent Puget Sound vintages have produced pleasing wines of great character, with some depth and complexity.

Sparkling Wines. Wines in which carbon dioxide is suspended, making them bubbly. Sparkling wines were invented in Champagne, France's northernmost wine district. Grapes in this area tend to be on the acidic side, because they don't always ripen fully. For this reason, sparkling wines have traditionally been naturally tart, even austere. Since the term Champagne designates a region of origin, it should not be used for American sparkling wines; in fact, it is illegal to use the term in Oregon and British Columbia, though not in Washington. The top Northwest sparkling wines are in no way inferior to French ones.

Sparkling wines are traditionally made from pinot noir (and in France from meunier as well) and from chardonnay grapes. In Washington, Riesling grapes may also be used. Sparkling wines with 1.5 percent residual sugar or less are labeled *brut;* those with 1.2–2 percent, *extra dry;* those with 1.7–3.5 percent, *sec;* those with 3.5–5 percent, *demi-sec;* and those with more than 5 percent, *doux;* A sparkling wine to which no dosage has been added will be bone dry and may be called *extra-brut* or *natural.*

Good sparkling wine will always be expensive because a great amount of work goes into making it.

Sparkling wines made in the traditional, time-consuming fashion may be labeled *méthode champenoise* or wine "fermented in this bottle." But read carefully. There is also a sparkling wine labeled wine "made in the bottle," and there is a great difference in methodology here between *this* and *the.* The latter is sparkling wine made by the simpler, cheaper transfer process, in which the sediments are filtered out. Filtered wines are less complex and their bubbles more sparingly distributed.

Sugar. Occurring naturally in grapes, sugar is the food the yeasts digest to make alcohol. The higher the sugar of the grape, the higher the potential alcohol of the wine. Fermentation stops when all the sugar has been digested or when the alcohol level becomes high enough (15 to 16 percent) to kill off the yeasts. In France it is legal to add sugar to unfermented grape juice in order to raise the alcohol level of a wine; in Washington, as in California and Oregon, it is not.

Syrah. A red-wine grape from France's hot-climate Rhône region, it produces the best wine when grown in austere soils; it loses its noble qualities when the vines are planted in fertile, irrigated bottomlands. At its best, the wine made from this grape

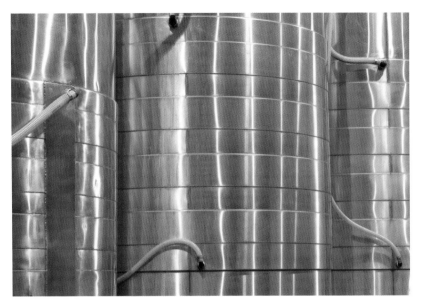

Stainless-steel fermenters help keep white wines fresh and preserve delicate flavors and aromas.

is big-bodied and complex and needs to be aged to bring out its best qualities. Plantings in Washington are quite recent, but they are increasing because this grape can make excellent wine, especially in the Yakima and Walla Walla Valleys and the Horse Heaven Hills.

Table Wine. A wine that has at least 7 percent but not more than 14 percent alcohol by volume. Wines so labeled need not state their exact alcohol content on the label. (The term is sometimes used, incorrectly, by consumers to denote an inexpensive wine.)

Tank. A very large container, usually upright and cylindrical, in which wine is fermented and stored. Tanks are commonly made of stainless steel, though they may also be made of wood or concrete (the latter are usually straight-sided cubicles) and lined with glass.

Tannins. Naturally occurring compounds in grape skins, seeds, and stems and in barrel oak that taste astringent and make the mouth pucker. Because tannins settle out in the natural sediments red wine throws as it ages, older reds have fewer tannins than do younger ones.

Tartaric Acid, Tartrates. The principal acid of wine, some of which is deposited in the form of crystals (tartrates) as the wine settles in a cask. Sometimes, in unstable wines, tartrates are also deposited in the bottle, and since they look like tiny shards of glass (though they are not harmful), consumers may complain of "broken glass" in the wine.

Terroir. The French term for soil, used to indicate that the soil of a specific vineyard imparts a special taste to its grapes and, through them, to the finished wine. The term is also used—colloquially, and not altogether correctly—to indicate a specific microclimate.

Varietal Wine. A wine that takes its name not from a town, district, or vineyard—as in much of Europe—but from the grape variety from which it is made, such as chardonnay, merlot, or sangiovese. According to law, at least 75 percent of a wine labeled as a varietal must be made from the grape variety printed on the label.

Vat. A large container of stainless steel, wood, or concrete, often open at the top, in which wine is fermented or blended. The term is sometimes used interchangeably with "tank."

Vertical Tasting. A tasting of one or more varietal wines of different vintages, but from the same winery or region, generally starting with the youngest and proceeding to the oldest.

Vinifera. The great wine grapes of the Old World, which—despite their widely varying character—all belong to a single species, *Vitis vinifera.* Many varieties of vinifera grapes have been successfully transplanted to the New World, and they produce our best wines. The native grapes of the New World tend to have odd flavors.

Vintage. The grape harvest, and the year in which the grapes are harvested. On the West Coast, the term "crush" may also be used for the harvest. A vintage date on a bottle always indicates the year in which the grapes were harvested—never the year in which the wine was bottled.

Viognier. A white-wine grape of France's Rhône Valley that gives a unique, distinguished golden wine with a fruity bouquet. Viognier grown in Columbia, Walla Walla, and Yakima Valley vineyards gives excellent fragrant wine with a good acid backbone.

Viticultural Area. *See* American Viticultural Area.

Walla Walla Valley AVA. An appellation encompassing the valley of the Walla Walla River in Washington and Oregon. Because of its deep, well-drained soils and benign climate, the region produces some of Washington's most complex and intense cabernet sauvignon, cabernet franc, and merlot grapes. The number of wineries in the valley has mushroomed in recent years as local wines have earned national accolades.

Woody. A pejorative term, said of a wine that has been stored in a wooden barrel or cask for too long and has picked up excessive wooden aromas and flavors—so excessive that, in some cases, it no longer tastes of grapes. It has the mouth feel you get when you've chewed on a wooden toothpick for too long.

Yeasts. Minute single-celled fungi that germinate and multiply rapidly as they feed on grape sugars, creating alcohol with the help of enzymes and releasing carbon dioxide. Because different yeasts vary in quality and flavor, winemakers must exercise care in their selection. The yeast cells die after fermentation—after they have run out of food—and slowly drift to the bottom of the wine barrel, where they make up a part of the lees left behind when the wine is racked or filtered.

Zinfandel. A red-wine grape especially popular on the West Coast. Much has been written about its origin, but even though scientists have traced it to an obscure Croatian grape, winemakers agree that the American variety has unique qualities and makes better wine than its European ancestor. Whatever its origin, this grape can give complex, well-balanced wine that ages as well as the best French clarets. This hot-climate grape variety has been planted successfully in Washington's Yakima Valley and, more recently, on bluffs of the Columbia Gorge, where it gives big, powerful wines.

VINTAGES: 1989–2003

Vintage charts are like guideposts: they show us the direction of travel, but they don't warn us about steep drops in the road, potholes, or washouts. This is especially true for the Pacific Northwest, which may be all of a piece politically and culturally but does not have geographic homogeneity. There are greater differences between vintages in Washington State than between vintages anywhere in California, because the soils and microclimates of this complex region differ as widely from each other as those of the Napa Valley do from the Loire Valley. Keep in mind also that Washington's wine industry is still so young that, in most cases, we don't really know yet whether a wine that shows problems as it ages is truly over the hill or just going through an awkward phase. But we're learning. In the meantime, below are some provisional notes.

1989 This was a truly great year for Columbia Valley and Yakima Valley reds. The grapes ripened to perfection, and a long autumn harvest, with hot days and cool nights, provided good fruit and firm acidity. The resulting wines were distinguished by balance and complexity. Cabernet sauvignon and merlot from the better wineries have realized their full potential, but the best can age for a few more years.

1990 An excellent vintage statewide, but even the biggest reds are now mature and beginning to fade.

1991 An initially underrated vintage showed how little we knew about Washington wines, because it turned out that many great ones took a long time to reach their peak. All are now mature, though many reds are so well balanced, with such depth and complexity, that they can still improve for a few more years.

1992 A severe winter freeze reduced the expected crop by half—average yields were only four tons per acre. The summer was long and hot, the harvest cool with some rain. Even so, the vintage's big cabernet sauvignons are still alive and kicking—as are a handful of its powerful reserve chardonnays.

1993 In eastern Washington an uncommonly cool summer and a long, warm fall brought about a long harvest with ripe fruit of uneven quality. Whites fared best. Some big high-extract wines (wines made from fully ripened fruit and left on the lees for a while before bottling) took a long time to evolve, but most reds have been ready to drink for quite some time, and some are beyond their peak. The Columbia Valley produced rather tannic reds, which matured a few years ago; the best can age for several more. The vintage's lean and crisp chardonnays have aged well but should be drunk soon. Surprisingly, a few late-harvest Rieslings are still holding their own.

1994 A warm, sunny harvest season ripened grapes to perfection. Yields were down, because the spring had been cool, but the reduced crop translated into more concentrated and intense wines. Columbia and Yakima Valley cabernet sauvignon, merlot, and nebbiolo from this excellent vintage have matured, though most are so well balanced that they were already splendid shortly after their release.

Washington's wine industry is young, so it's difficult to tell if a wine that is showing problems as it ages is over the hill or just going through an awkward phase.

1995 Washington fared well in a difficult vintage, with a cool wet summer followed by a marvelous autumn. The interior valleys produced complex, age-worthy reds, particularly cabernet sauvignon, merlot, and syrah. Some late-harvest Rieslings were also fine and can age for a few more years.

1996 A difficult year. A severe frost hit eastern Washington during the winter, affecting the quantity of wine, especially reds, and cutting yields by 50 percent for the next several vintages. Most of the 1996 reds, and some of the whites, are still holding up well.

1997 To everybody's surprise, the vine-damaging frosts of the 1996–1997 winter had little effect on the quality of the wines. After the frosts came a warm spring, a hot summer, and a long, wet, cool harvest throughout the state; drying winds helped keep grapes free of rot. Overall, the quality was high. Washington nebbiolo from 1997 is still young and, while it's enjoyable now, it can age for several more years. Many of the big reds are just beginning to wake up; before you decide to age any of them for much longer, taste them. A few well-made Yakima Valley and Columbia Gorge chardonnays from this vintage are still improving, but most are showing their age and beginning to fade. Sémillon and sauvignon blanc have quietly passed away, but a few Rieslings are still hale and hearty.

1998 After a long, hot summer with record temperatures in eastern Washington, came a long, warm autumn, which yielded big, deeply colored, powerful reds, notably cabernet sauvignon and syrah; they're enjoyable now but may be aged for a few more years. Taste a bottle before you lay away a case, since there's quite a bit of variation in aging potential. Chardonnay, Riesling, sauvignon blanc, sémillon, viognier, and merlot from this vintage were also excellent but should have been consumed by now. Surprisingly, some 1998 Yakima Valley chenin blanc is still holding up nicely. Well-made Yakima Valley late-harvest Rieslings can age for a few more years.

1999 Flowering happened on schedule, but because grapes need warm weather to become fertilized, cool weather early in the season led to a smaller than normal set of fruit. But a hot September and October allowed the grapes to reach ideal maturity levels. All of this created the best Washington whites of the decade. Most of the lighter reds—lemberger, sangiovese, and some pinot noir—are past their

prime (though there may be a few surprises lurking in the cellar), but cabernet, nebbiolo, syrah, zinfandel, and even some merlot can benefit from further aging.

2000 The autumn of 2000 was an unusual one: in the Columbia, Yakima, and Walla Walla Valleys, the nights stayed very mild far into the season, and trees glowed with fall colors for weeks rather than days. The grapes kept their acid levels, yielding wines of good structure and aging potential, especially the reds. The lighter reds and whites from this vintage are beyond their prime, yet the best of the pinot noirs and chardonnays are still very much alive. A few solidly structured Rieslings are ready to drink now but could age a bit more. The same is true for Yakima Valley sémillon, which has aged beautifully. This was the first year in which Washington produced more red wine than white.

2001 An uncommonly dry winter in eastern Washington preceded a dry spring, but enough rain fell in June and August to moisten the soil in the few unirrigated vineyards. Irrigation water was rationed, and some it was cut off in mid-September, especially along the Roza Canal. But the vines seemed unaffected, carrying so much fruit that some growers had to thin the clusters. The combination of low moisture and hot weather raised sugars quickly, forcing some growers to harvest the fruit early to prevent over-ripeness, as California growers often have to do. Harvest began in mid to late September, a week or two earlier than usual. But some of the grapes thus harvested, before their acids and flavors could develop, produced flabby wines, high in alcohol, that may not age well; time will tell. It was, however, a good vintage for Puget Sound, where a cool summer kept sugar levels down.

2002 This was a great vintage for Puget Sound vineyards just coming into production. White-wine grapes like siegerrebe and madeleine angevine yielded very appealing wines of surprising depth. In eastern Washington, a cool spring meant lower yields but more intense fruit; that intensity was heightened when cool weather struck in late September, delaying the ripening of those grapes still on the vines. (In the hottest areas, grapes had already ripened and were harvested in early September.) Judging by some of the whites that have already been released, this could turn out to be an excellent vintage.

2003 An unexpected cold spell in April set back the grapes and delayed flowering, but as I write it's too early to tell what the result will be.

I N D E X

COMPASS AMERICAN GUIDES

Compass American Guides are available at special discounts for bulk purchases for sales promotions or premiums. Special editions, including personalized covers, excerpts of existing guides, and corporate imprints, can be created in large quantities for special needs. For more information, write to Special Markets/Premium Sales, 1745 Broadway, MD 6-2, New York, New York 10019, or e-mail specialmarkets@randomhouse.com. Inquiries from Canada should be directed to your local Canadian bookseller or sent to Random House of Canada, Ltd., Marketing Department, 2775 Matheson Boulevard East, Mississauga, Ontario L4W 4P7. Inquiries from the United Kingdom should be sent to Fodor's Travel Publications, 20 Vauxhall Bridge Road, London, England SW1V 2SA.

COMPASS AMERICAN GUIDES

Critics, booksellers, and travelers all agree: you're lost without a Compass.

"This splendid series provides exactly the sort of historical and cultural detail about North American destinations that curious-minded travelers need."
—*Washington Post*

"This is a series that constantly stuns us...no guide with photos this good should have writing this good. But it does." —*New York Daily News*

"Of the many guidebooks on the market, few are as visually stimulating, as thoroughly researched, or as lively written as the Compass American Guide series."
—*Chicago Tribune*

"Good to read ahead of time, then take along so you don't miss anything."
—*San Diego Magazine*

"Magnificent photography. First rate."—*Money*

"Written by longtime residents of each destination...these handsome and literate guides are strong on history and culture, and illustrated with gorgeous photos."
—*San Francisco Chronicle*

"The color photographs sparkle, the archival illustrations illuminate windows to the past, and the writing is usually of the utmost caliber." —*Michigan Tribune*

"Class acts, worth reading and shelving for keeps even if you're not a traveler. "
—*New Orleans Times-Picayune*

"Beautiful photographs and literate writing are the hallmarks of the Compass guides." —*Nashville Tennessean*

"History, geography, and wanderlust converge in these well-conceived books."
—*Raleigh News & Observer*

"Oh, my goodness! What a gorgeous series this is."—*Booklist*

ACKNOWLEDGMENTS

■ FROM THE AUTHOR

Much thanks to the winemakers on both sides of the Cascade Mountains who have welcomed me into Washington wineries for more than two decades, and especially to Mike Wallace of Hinzerling Winery and Clay Mackey and Kay Simon of Chinook Wines, both in Prosser, whose wines first alerted me to the fact that Washington State can indeed produce world-class wines; to Doug Charles of Compass Wines, in Anacortes, whose insights illuminated the ins and outs of the wine trade; to Daniel Mangin, for walking that extra mile to make sure this book happened; to Craig Seligman, for doing such a great job editing it; and to Tina Malaney and Fabrizio La Rocca for their very fine design work.

■ FROM THE PUBLISHER

Compass American Guides would like to thank John Morrone for copyediting the manuscript, Ellen Klages for proofreading it, and Joan Stout for indexing it. All photographs in this book are by Greg Vaughn unless noted below. Compass American Guides would like to thank the following individuals or institutions for the use of their illustrations or photographs:

TABLE OF CONTENTS
Page 6, ©Brent Bergherm

INTRODUCTION
Pages 8–9, ©Brent Bergherm; page 10, MSCUA, University of Washington Libraries (NA 4171); page 13, Museum of History and Industry, Seattle (SHS 7294); page 16, ©Brent Bergherm

THE SETTING
Page 20, Museum of History and Industry, Seattle (SHS 6637); pages 26–27, ©Brent Bergherm

STEPPING INTO HISTORY
Pages 32–33, Yakima Valley Museum; page 35, Washington State Tourism (J. Poth); pages 36–37, Washington State Historical Society (34061); page 41,

Washington State Historical Society; pages 42–43, Yakima Valley Museum; page 45 (top), MSCUA, University of Washington Libraries (UW5204); page 45 (bottom), MSCUA, University of Washington Libraries (UW230552)

Food and Wine
Pages 54–55, MSCUA, University of Washington Libraries (UW6654); page 58, Patit Creek Restaurant; page 60, Herbfarm Restaurant

Geology, Climate, Landscape
Pages 63, ©Brent Bergherm; pages 66–67, ©Brent Bergherm

Visiting Wineries
Page 73, ©Brent Bergherm; pages 84–85, ©Brent Bergherm

Puget Sound and the Southern Lowlands
Page 98, Museum of History and Industry, Seattle (SHS 7295); page 105, *Seattle Times*; page 110, MSCUA ,University of Washington Libraries (UW10286); page 117, Pasek Cellars

Yakima Valley
Page 132, Yakima Valley Regional Library; pages 134–135, Yakima Valley Museum; page 136 (top), Yakima Valley Museum; page 140 Yakima Valley Museum; page 142, Yakima Valley Museum; page 154, Yakima Valley Winery Association (Russ Dix)

Columbia Valley and the Tri-Cities
Pages 168-169, MSCUA, University of Washington Libraries (DAM063)

Walla Walla Valley
Page 179, ©Brent Bergherm; pages 180–181, ©Brent Bergherm; page 182, MSCUA, University of Washington Libraries (NA4169); pages 186–187, ©BrentBergherm/Fotostock; pages 194–195, courtesy of C. Schmitt

Vintages 1989–2003
Page 241, Yakima Valley Winery Association

■ ABOUT THE AUTHOR

John Doerper has worked as a food and wine columnist and editor for numerous publications. His articles about food, wine, and travel have appeared in *Travel & Leisure* and *Pacific Northwest Magazine,* among others. An artist and avid gardener, John is the author of several Compass American Guides—*California Wine Country, Coastal California, Oregon Wine Country, Pacific Northwest,* and *Washington.* He lives in Bellingham, Washington.

■ ABOUT THE PHOTOGRAPHER

Greg Vaughn's award-winning imagery has appeared in *National Geographic, Outside, National Wildlife, Sierra, Natural History,* and *Travel & Leisure,* and he was the principal photographer for the Compass American Guides *Oregon* and *Washington* as well as *Oregon Wine Country.*